Preschool ABC's
Assessment, Behavior & Classroom Management

Carson-Dellosa Publishing LLC
Greensboro, North Carolina

Note that some activities in this book may present safety issues. Before beginning the activities, ask families' permission and inquire about the following:

- children's food allergies and religious or other food restrictions.
- possible latex allergies.
- children's scent sensitivities and/or allergies.

Also, remember that uninflated or popped balloons may present a choking hazard.

Finally, note that exercise activities may require adult supervision. Children should always warm up prior to beginning any exercise activity and should stop immediately if they feel any discomfort during exercise.

Credits

Content Editor: Joanie Oliphant

Copy Editor: Beatrice Allen

Layout Design: Lori Jackson

Carson-Dellosa Publishing LLC
PO Box 35665
Greensboro, NC 27425 USA
www.carsondellosa.com

ISBN 978-1-936024-85-8

335107784

Table of Contents

Preschool ABC's: **A**ssessment, **B**ehavior & **C**lassroom Management is for early childhood educators working with children during the exciting, challenging, and joyful preschool years. The intention of this book is to inspire educators to tailor the approaches and lessons as they teach and care for young children. While creating an environment that supports program curriculum goals and individual children's interests and abilities, educators must design effective solutions for assessment, behavior, and classroom management. *Preschool ABC's* provides the strategies necessary for success in the early childhood classroom.

Assessment

With the assessment tools included, growth and development of children can be tracked and used to plan specific activities that promote continued learning. With consistent assessment of progress and achievement, a clear picture is drawn of each child's strengths and challenges. Using results from assessment helps in lesson planning by directing plans to match needs and encourage growth in each child's development. This section provides a number of checklists, assessment activities, and developmental milestones. It is separated into two age groups: Toddlers (ages 18–36 months) and Preschoolers (ages 3–5 years). Each age group focuses on four developmental areas:

- Social and Emotional Development: how children express who they are, and how they interact with other children and adults.

- Language Development: how children communicate as they develop receptive language, expressive language, and conversational skills.

- Cognitive Development: how children explore, reason, imagine, understand concepts, and solve problems.

- Physical Development: how children move and use their bodies to accomplish various activities.

Behavior

Educators can prepare children for classroom success by establishing an effective behavior management strategy. This section will provide ideas for positive ways to influence behavior and ways to minimize problems and behavior issues as they arise.

Discipline: The key to a successful discipline strategy is knowing how to combine the concepts of safety, respect for self and others, and expectations of appropriate behavior so that children feel loved, valued, safe, and responsible. This section provides alternative disciplinary techniques, behavior management strategies, and guidelines for minimizing discipline problems.

Each of the next four specific behavior sections, Anger Management, Sharing, Patience, and Self-Regulation, will provide varied and flexible tools that can be implemented as each program year begins. Develop and apply the activities, songs, children's literature recommendations, sample letters home, and checklists according to children's needs.

Classroom Management

Developing an effective classroom management strategy will help you prepare for success before the first day of school begins. This section includes everyday Strategies for Success, from tips for room arrangement to routines and consistency.

Solutions Throughout the Day: A predictable daily plan will go a long way toward achieving success in an early childhood classroom. Transitions, soothing activities, snack time, and suggested rules for the classroom, lunchtime, playground, bathroom, and nap time are featured.

ABCs of Common Behaviors: Behavior problems, from aggressive play to whining, are addressed. Each topic is addressed with the psychology behind the behavior, specific management ideas for improving the behavior, and suggestions for engaging the whole class in learning appropriate behavior choices.

The Challenge Years: Some program years are more challenging than others! Be encouraged by these proven strategies.

Teaming with Families: Inviting families to participate in their children's education offers lasting benefits to the child, family, classroom, and the entire program.

Social and Emotional Development

While two-year-olds' physical growth slows considerably compared to their growth rate as infants, the social and emotional changes are tremendous. Toddlers begin to assert some independence but are still very reliant on the comfort and security offered by those in charge. Two-year-olds start to recognize that there are rules that must be obeyed, so they begin to develop a small amount of self-control. By nature, toddlers and two-year-olds are self-centered. They are concerned almost exclusively with their own needs and wants, and their ability to understand how others might feel has yet to be developed. This sometimes leads family members and caregivers to fear that a child is spoiled, but it is all part of a child's natural development.

Social Development

If you have ever tried to encourage a group of toddlers to share a set of toys, you were probably faced with a host of unpleasant reactions. Because toddlers and two-year-olds are mostly concerned about their own desires, it is very difficult for them to share and to play with other children. A toddler may not have the capacity to understand that her behaviors affect others. Despite this self-centeredness, toddlers spend a great deal of their playtime imitating others. While two-year-olds pretend to read favorite bedtime stories to their teddy bears or dolls, they sound exactly like the family member or caregiver who reads to them. They imitate the actions and words of their family members while they pretend to work, cook, garden, and keep house. Through pretending, children begin to learn important social skills.

Emotional Development

Mood swings are a hallmark of a two-year-old's emotional life. One minute, a child is happy and playful; the next, he is angry and sulking. This emotional roller coaster is a sign of a child's struggles to understand his impulses and feelings. Frustration is another common emotion experienced by children of this age. They want to test their limits and explore their world beyond what most adults find acceptable. Because they lack the skills to keep themselves safe during their explorations, toddlers and two-year-olds often react with anger when pulled back within acceptable boundaries. Temper tantrums, hitting, biting, screaming, or kicking are all part of the normal behavior for children this age. Despite these more challenging traits, a toddler or a two-year-old's warm hug and delightful smile come easily, and affection is openly shared. Consistent and reasonable limits need to be set for a child so that exploration and independence can develop in a safe environment.

Social and Emotional Development

Benchmarks of Social Development

- Uses "pretend" play to understand the world

- Imitates others

- Wants to explore surroundings

- Fluctuates between wanting and not wanting more independence

- Begins development of self-regulation

- Begins to understand social rules

- Takes turns in games

- Focuses on personal needs and wants

- Has difficulty sharing

- Understands "mine" and "yours"

- Plays side by side with other children instead of with them

- Tests limits and boundaries

Benchmarks of Emotional Development

- Easily expresses affection

- Begins sensing how others feel

- Experiences a wide range of emotions

- Takes pride in accomplishments

- Has difficulty adjusting to major changes in routines

- Needs to have consistent, reasonable limits enforced

This book provides generalized descriptions of expected development. All children develop at their own pace and in their own way. Recommend that families contact a pediatrician if children show any of the following signs of delayed social and emotional development:

- Does not engage in "pretend" play

- Cannot understand one-step instructions, such as "Bring me the ball."

- Cannot communicate using short, simple phrases

- Does not show any interest in other children

- Has an extremely difficult time being separated from primary caregiver

Activities to Assess Social and Emotional Development

Make a copy of the Assessment Checklist on page 9 for each child that you plan to assess. Use the checklist to record your observations of the child as she participates in the following activities. Repeat your assessments periodically to determine her growth.

All About Me

Ask the child the following questions to determine if he knows basic personal information:

- What is your name?

- How old are you?

- Can you show me your favorite _____?

- What are your family members' names?

- Do you have any brothers or sisters?

Drama Time

Invite the child to select dolls or stuffed animals and bring them to the dramatic play area of the classroom. Encourage her to act out various scenarios with the toys, such as going to the grocery store, playing at the park, eating dinner at home, and spending a day at school. Allow her interests to dictate the imaginary play. Only join in the play if you are invited to do so. Make a note of the roles the child assumes and how she interacts with the toys.

Hello, Good-Bye

When the child arrives at school, observe how he reacts. Does he cling to the family member and cry? Does he enter the room confidently? Does he express affection to the caregivers in the room? Does he engage in play with other children, or does he seek solitary activities? Record your observations on the checklist. At the end of the day, watch the child's reaction to the family member who arrives to take him home. Is the reunion happy? Does the child cry? Does he show or tell the family about his day? Again, record your observations on the checklist. Think about ways that you can build trust with him to improve the transitions during arrival and departure times.

Playground Pals

During outdoor playtime, watch how the child interacts with other children. Does she play alone, beside others, or with others? Does she show knowledge of basic social rules, such as sharing, cooperating, and taking turns? What activities does she choose to participate in? Are the activities solitary or group-oriented? Think about ways to encourage social skills based on her developmental ability to interact with others.

Assessment Checklist for Social and Emotional Development

Child's Name _____ Age _____

Observer _____ Date _____

Activities Observed _____

	Not Observed	Demonstrates Little Ability	Demonstrates Some Ability	Demonstrates Proficiency	Comments
Self-Expression					
Tells name and age					
Tells about family					
Identifies favorite things					
Responds appropriately to questions					
Imitates others					
Shows pride in accomplishments					
Acts independently					
Demonstrates self-confidence					
Chooses activities based on personal interests					
Participates in imaginary play					
Assumes a variety of roles					
Interactions with Adults					
Trusts adults outside of the family					
Talks with adults outside of the family					
Separates easily from family members					
Talks with family members					
Expresses affection					
Interactions with Other Children					
Shows interest in other children					
Plays alone					
Plays beside others					
Plays with others					
Behaves cooperatively					
Takes turns					
Shares					

Language Development

From their second birthdays to their third, toddlers rapidly increase their vocabularies. At the beginning of this time period, two-year-olds typically have vocabularies of 50 or more words. By the time they reach the age of three, they have vocabularies of 300 or more words. It is important to remember that the differences between individual children at this age are extremely varied. Some toddlers develop language skills steadily, while others seem to make gains in stop-and-go bursts. Highly verbal children are not necessarily more intelligent than their quieter counterparts, nor are their vocabularies necessarily stronger. They are just more apt to express themselves. Generally speaking, girls at this age tend to be more verbal than boys, but by the time they reach kindergarten the differences usually even out.

Receptive Language

Receptive language is the comprehension of words, actions and gestures, directions, and questions. Two-year-olds are capable of understanding almost everything that is said to them and they can usually follow simple commands that involve two or three different directions. For example, they will understand what to do if they are told to clean up their toys, wash their hands, and sit for lunch. At this age, two-year-olds can also follow the story line of a book and remember details, story sequences, ideas, and bits of information gleaned from books. Because their attention spans are still limited, books that are shared with two-year-olds should be short and activity-oriented. Books that encourage children to mimic sounds, repeat phrases, and name objects can be especially useful in developing language.

Expressive Language

Expressive language is the use of words, actions and gestures, and the expression of thoughts and ideas. Two-year-olds communicate using two- or three-word sentences. By the end of this year, they will use sentences of up to six words. Two-year-olds begin using pronouns such as *I*, *you*, *me*, and *we*, and they understand the concepts of "mine" and "his/hers." A two-year-old can say her own name, age, and gender. Unlike a younger toddler, whose speech can be indecipherable to anyone but family, strangers are likely to understand the words used by a two-year-old.

Conversational Skills

Through listening to adult conversations and practicing their own, toddlers begin to learn many of the basic rules of grammar. They also learn the give-and-take of having conversations—alternating between listening and speaking. Children at this age may have difficulty understanding when it is their turn to speak and when it is not, so interruptions in other people's conversations may be common. Gentle reminders about taking turns and engaging toddlers in frequent conversations will help children develop stronger communication skills.

Benchmarks of Language Development

- Begins this time period with a spoken vocabulary of 50 or more words

- Ends this time period with a spoken vocabulary of 300 or more words

- Has strong receptive language skills—understands almost everything that is said

- Understands and follows simple commands involving two to three different directions

- Remembers details, story sequences, ideas, and bits of information gleaned from books

- Enjoys mimicking sounds

- Names almost all common objects

- Begins this time period using two- and three-word sentences

- Ends this time period using up to six-word sentences

- Uses pronouns in speech

- Understands the concepts of "mine" and "his/hers"

- Has developed speech that is understandable to strangers

- Begins to understand basic grammar rules through listening to and practicing conversations

- Begins to learn social rules for conversations—alternating between listening and speaking

This book provides generalized descriptions of expected development. All children develop at their own paces and in their own ways. Recommend that families contact a pediatrician if children show any of the following signs of delayed language development:

- Speech is unclear or indecipherable to non-family members

- Cannot understand simple instructions

- Cannot communicate using short, simple phrases

Activities to Assess Language Development

Make a copy of the Assessment Checklist on page 13 for each child that you plan to assess. Use the checklist to record your observations of the child as she participates in the following activities. Repeat your assessments periodically to determine her growth.

Teacher Says

Play a game of "Teacher Says" with the child. Tell him that in this game, he is to follow your commands. Start with one command at a time, such as "Teacher says—pat your tummy." Watch to see if he understands the command and executes it. After several single commands, increase the difficulty by adding a second command: "Teacher says—touch your toes, then tap your nose." Continue to increase the number of commands until you reach his limit. Make a note on the assessment checklist about how many commands the child could follow and what types of vocabulary words he understood. If there were words that the child did not understand, note them as well. Think of ways to help him enrich his vocabulary.

What's Next?

Invite the child to select a favorite storybook that she has heard several times. Read a few pages of the story and then say, "What's next?" Have her tell you what she remembers about what happens next in the story. Read a few more pages and congratulate her on any of the details that she remembered. Continue to stop reading after every few pages and ask, "What's next?" Record your observations on the checklist. What types of words does she use to describe the story? Are the details accurate? Does she use pronouns appropriately?

Ring, Ring

For this activity, you need two play phones—one for you and one for the child. Have him sit back-to-back with you and pretend to answer the phone when you say "Ring, ring." Elicit a conversation with him by asking about his day, a favorite book or movie, or a favorite activity. Notice his ability to participate in a conversation. Does he take turns talking and listening? Is his speech understandable? Does he demonstrate knowledge of basic grammar rules? Record your observations on the checklist.

Assessment Checklist for Language Development

Child's Name _____ Age _____

Observer _____ Date _____

Activities Observed _____

	Not Observed	Demonstrates Little Ability	Demonstrates Some Ability	Demonstrates Proficiency	Comments
Receptive Language					
Follows single commands					
Follows two- or three-part commands					
Follows more than a three-part command					
Knows vocabulary words related to _____					
Knows vocabulary words related to _____					
Recalls story details					
Expressive Language					
Uses two- and three-word sentences					
Uses four- and five-word sentences					
Uses sentences with six or more words					
Uses pronouns					
Speech is understandable					
Speech is grammatically appropriate					
Tells about story details					
Can say own name, age, and gender					
Pronounces words correctly					
Conversation Skills					
Participates in conversations					
Alternates between listening and speaking					

Cognitive Development

Cognitive abilities relate to memory, intellect, problem solving, and imagination. Infants and toddlers learn about the world through their senses—by touching, tasting, listening, and watching.

Two-year-olds begin to learn about the world by thinking. They begin to understand relationships between objects and can clearly see similarities and differences between things. They are able to match objects that are the same and can sort objects that are different by color, shape, and size.

Two-year-olds can think about and predict cause and effect relationships—for example, after some experience at the water table, children this age may be able to predict that heavier objects will cause larger splashes than lighter objects when dropped into the water.

Two-year-olds develop a rudimentary sense of time and can understand concepts such as "now" and "later." They may be able to describe events that took place yesterday and events that are supposed to happen tomorrow.

Counting skills are limited at this age, but two-year-olds generally understand what "one" and "two" mean. Imaginative play becomes increasingly complex as the children learn to put together longer sequences of events, and their abilities to focus on one activity at a time deepen.

Caregivers and family members recognize that two-year-olds have great difficulty understanding reason. Because children at this age have self-centered views of the world, they do not understand how others feel or think. They are not capable of listening to and comprehending long, drawn-out explanations. Another challenge is that two-year-olds often think that their behaviors directly impact everything that happens around them. For example, if a pet is hurt by a car, the two-year-old likely believes that she caused the accident. Because of this, it is very important that adults assure two-year-olds that they are not responsible for events such as illness, death, and divorce.

Benchmarks of Cognitive Development

- Understands relationships between objects

- Sees similarities and differences between objects

- Matches objects that are the same

- Sorts objects by color, size, and shape

- Completes simple puzzles with whole-object pieces

- Thinks about and predicts cause and effect relationships

- Understands "now" and "later"

- Tells about things that happened yesterday and things that will happen tomorrow

- Counts to two with understanding of number concept

- Increases complexity of imaginative play

- Has difficulty understanding reason

- Believes that his or her actions impact everything in the world

This book provides generalized descriptions of expected development. All children develop at their own pace and in their own way. Recommend that families contact a pediatrician if children show any of the following signs of delayed cognitive development:

- Does not engage in "pretend" play

- Cannot understand simple instructions

- Cannot communicate using short, simple phrases

- Speech is unclear or indecipherable

Activities to Assess Cognitive Development

Make a copy of the Assessment Checklist on page 17 for each child that you plan to assess. Use the checklist to record your observations of the child as he participates in the following activities. Repeat your assessments periodically to determine the child's growth.

Match Up

For this activity, you need two square tissue boxes and two copies each of six different pictures. Choose an interesting theme for the pictures, such as toys, vehicles, or animals, and select pictures that children will be able to name. Tape each cardboard box closed. Then, tape one set of pictures to the six faces of the first box and the matching pictures to the faces of the second box. Invite the child to toss both boxes into the air (one at a time, if necessary). When the boxes land on the ground, have her name each picture showing at the tops of the boxes and tell you if they match. Record your observations on the checklist.

Count the Stickers

Staple six large index cards together to make a booklet. Number the pages from one to six. Select stickers that will be interesting to children and place the appropriate number of stickers on each page. For example, use one dog sticker for number one, two cat stickers for number two, and so on. Invite the child to count the stickers on each page. Use the assessment checklist to note which numbers he was able to recognize and how far he was able to count.

Puzzled

Select two or more puzzles that feature whole-object pieces. Make sure that the selected puzzles feature different themes, such as one with fruits and another with animals. Place all of the puzzle pieces together in a paper bag and set the puzzle boards on a table. Invite the child to empty the contents of the bag and sort the pieces into the appropriate categories. Then, invite her to complete each puzzle. Watch how she approaches the tasks of sorting the pieces and completing the puzzles. Does she seem to apply any particular strategies? Note your observations on the checklist. Think of ways to further develop the child's problem-solving skills.

Assessment Checklist for Cognitive Development

Child's Name _____ Age _____

Observer _____ Date _____

Activities Observed _____

	Not Observed	Demonstrates Little Ability	Demonstrates Some Ability	Demonstrates Proficiency	Comments
Matches objects that are the same					
Identifies similarities and differences between objects					
Sorts objects by color, size, and shape					
Sorts objects by theme					
Identifies numbers					
Counts to _____					
Names objects					
Completes puzzles					
Asks questions					
Names colors					
Predicts cause and effect relationships					
Participates in imaginative play					
Understands "now" and "later"					
Tells about past and future events					

Physical Development

Toddlers seem to be constantly on the go. They run, jump, kick, climb, and ride tricycles. The high level of activity may seem exhausting to adults, but it helps children develop strength and coordination. As children move through this stage, the clumsiness that they demonstrated in the earlier toddler months begins to disappear. They begin to walk with a more adult-like heel-to-toe motion, rather than the spread-legged waddle of a young toddler. They run more smoothly and learn to walk up and down steps while holding on to a rail. Two-year-olds learn to kick balls and can sometimes even control the direction that the ball will move. Children this age can use their hands, talk, and look around while walking. They are able to walk backward and can sometimes stand on one leg with help. Two-year-olds benefit greatly from outdoor playtime when they can run and explore. But, keep in mind that their abilities to use good judgment are limited. It is up to adults to enforce safe and reasonable boundaries.

Two-year-olds also make great improvements with their fine motor skills. Give a child this age a box of crayons and he will not only be able to grasp it but also to use it to draw his first masterpieces. Two-year-olds can easily use small objects, turn the pages of a book, and build block towers with about six blocks. They can take off their own shoes and unzip large zippers. They can coordinate the use of the wrists, hands, and fingers well enough to be able to turn a doorknob, unwrap paper from a piece of candy, and unscrew the lid on a jar.

The development of physical coordination brings with it some ability for a child to attend to some basic self-care tasks. Two-year-olds are capable of using a spoon, drinking from a cup, and feeding themselves some finger foods. Children this age usually have all of their baby teeth, and they need to be taught good dental hygiene. While they will not be able to brush their teeth completely independently at this age, they can participate—allow children to use their toothbrushes on their own, but supervise closely to make sure that all of their teeth are cleaned, front and back, and that they do not swallow too much of the toothpaste. If toilet learning has not already started, most children are ready for it by the time they turn two. Toilet learning should always be approached in a relaxed, positive manner, and punishments for accidents should be avoided entirely. Learning to use the toilet becomes an important issue during the third year, especially as children see peers giving up diapers.

Benchmarks of Physical Development

- Runs well

- Walks backward

- Climbs easily

- Walks up and down stairs while holding on to a rail

- Rides a tricycle

- Kicks a ball

- Turns pages of a book

- Uses a pencil or crayon to draw vertical and horizontal lines and circles

- Builds block towers with up to six blocks

- Turns doorknobs and handles

- Screws and unscrews jar lids

- Unzips large zippers

- Takes off own shoes

- Uses a spoon to eat

- Self-feeds some finger foods

- Drinks from a cup

- Brushes teeth with help

- Shows interest and readiness in toileting

This book provides generalized descriptions of expected development. All children develop at their own pace and in their own way. Recommend that families contact a pediatrician if children show any of the following signs of delayed cognitive development:

- Has difficulty with stairs and often falls on them

- Cannot build a tower with more than four blocks

- Cannot manipulate small objects

- Cannot draw a circle while looking at a circle by the age of three

Activities to Assess Physical Development

Make a copy of the Assessment Checklist on page 21 for each child that you plan to assess. Use the checklist to record your observations of the child as he participates in the following activities. Repeat your assessments periodically to determine the child's growth.

Course of Action

Set up a simple obstacle course on the playground to assess the child's gross motor skills. Divide the course into sections so that you can observe her running, jumping, hopping, riding a tricycle, and climbing. Depending on her interests and abilities, you may want to have her complete only one or two sections of the course in a single session. Introduce the sections one at a time. If necessary, demonstrate the task for her. Watch the child as she runs to the fence and back, jumps in place, hops on one foot, rides a tricycle in a circle, and climbs on the play equipment. Does she move with ease, or does she struggle with the tasks? Are her movements fluid or jerky? Does the child show confidence in her ability to complete each task? Record your observations on the checklist.

Copy Cat

Set out two large sheets of drawing paper and a few crayons for you and the child. Draw a vertical line on your paper and invite the child to copy what you drew on his paper. Next, ask him to draw something for you to copy. Continue in this manner until he has had the chance to draw various lines, squares, and circles. Notice how he holds the crayon—in a fist, or with thumb and fingers on opposite sides? Was the child able to copy the shapes that you drew? Was he able to draw shapes for you to copy? Use the checklist to note your observations. Think about activities that you can develop to help the child increase his small-muscle coordination.

Tea Party

Invite the child to join you for a tea party. Have her help you set the table with plates, bowls, cups, utensils, and napkins. Set a pitcher of water, a tray of finger sandwiches, a bowl of warm soup, and some fruit salad on the table. Have the child select food for her plate and note how she uses the utensils. Can she use a spoon to eat the soup without spilling it? Does she use a fork to eat the fruit? If she is an older two-year-old, or is three years old, invite her to pour a cup of water from the pitcher. Does she accomplish this with little spilling? Make a note of your observations on the checklist.

 (See page 2.)

Assessment Checklist for Physical Development

Child's Name _____ Age _____

Observer _____ Date _____

Activities Observed _____

	Not Observed	Demonstrates Little Ability	Demonstrates Some Ability	Demonstrates Proficiency	Comments
Runs					
Jumps in place					
Hops on one foot					
Rides a tricycle					
Kicks a ball					
Catches bounced ball					
Throws ball overhand					
Walks up and down stairs					
Walks backward					
Turns pages of book					
Draws and copies shapes					
Holds crayon or pencil with thumb and fingers					
Builds block towers with blocks					
Unzips zippers					
Unbuttons buttons					
Uses scissors					
Draws a person with two to four body parts					
Strings beads					
Solves jigsaw puzzles					
Uses spoon to eat					
Uses fork to eat					
Pours water from pitcher					
Drinks from cup					

Social and Emotional Development

The social-emotional well-being of a child influences all other areas of his development. A child who feels self-confident, well liked, and secure is more likely to make cognitive steps in learning. A child who is insecure may have a harder time growing and learning. Family and the home life are the biggest factors in the child's social-emotional well-being. Family members who are too rushed to allow their child to attempt to put on his coat send a "you are not capable" message. The child who has been pushed around and bullied at home may bring the same actions into the classroom. Families that are patient and give verbal encouragement promote an attitude of "I can do anything" in their child. A child who has been taught by encouragement brings that attitude to other learning tasks.

It is up to you to accept the backgrounds (or differences) represented by the children in class and to create a safe, positive, nurturing environment where all children can learn. Model for children that every one of them is important to the class. No one child should receive the majority of your attention. The class should have rules to keep everyone safe, but not so many that children get bogged down with what they cannot do. It is best if the rules say what to do rather than what not to do.

Social development may be observed in the way children play in a group. They play together in the following progression:

- Solitary play: Solitary play is when a child plays alone, completely unaware of other children around her. This child is totally focused on what she is doing.

- Parallel play: Parallel play is when children play side by side with similar toys, but they have no interaction. A child may take smaller blocks to the block area and play beside other children playing there.

- Associative play: Associative play is when children begin to play with others. These children may play side by side and talk with one another, but they have different goals in their play. One may be building a road on which to drive a car; another may be building a tower to see how tall it will be.

- Cooperative play: Cooperative play involves playing with common ideas and negotiation. For example, both children plan to join the tower and the road. The children have mutual goals in the play, and they work together to attain the goals.

These are stages of play that children go through during their early years. In the classroom, you may have children at all four stages at one time. Your job is to help children work through the stages so that all children successfully arrive at "cooperative play."

Separation anxiety is another social-emotional stage that most children experience. Sometimes, when the stage is missed during the toddler years, it occurs during the preschool years. It worries family members when their child starts crying at the school entrance for no apparent reason. Family members may question the child to find out what the problem is at school, hoping to tell the teacher what needs to be fixed. The more the child is questioned, the more reasons he will produce: "I want to play with the red truck and never get a chance." "I don't want to paint today." These are examples of reasons a child may give the family member for crying at the door. The child cannot verbalize what his fear really is, which is, What if my family does not come back?

Remain calm and reassure the family member and child that school is enjoyable. Help direct him to an engaging task. Rather than discuss the issue of separation anxiety in front of the child, make an appointment to call the family member when the child is not present. It is best if family members understand that they should not linger in the classroom when the child is experiencing separation anxiety.

Most of the time, you assess social-emotional development by quietly observing children and writing brief notes on what you observe. To assess by this method, use the Anecdotal Note form found on page 27. Position yourself in an area near the child or children to be assessed, but not so close that you are a part of the group. Note who you are assessing, who is in the play group, what the children are doing and saying to each other, and what roles the children are taking (leader, follower, or onlooker). You can then place these pages in the child's file and compare them with other observations. Comparing them will show areas of growth and development of skills throughout the year. Your observations will show the rate of growth of the children learning to share and play cooperatively in a small group. You can observe if words are used consistently to negotiate or if some of the children are still hitting, pushing, or grabbing toys from others. This type of assessment also shows whether the children are playing truly interactive group games or whether there is one consistent leader. You can also observe progress in self-regulation and expression of emotions.

Occasionally, a child will demonstrate rapid growth. He may have the most exciting story to tell you. It may be an event that took place, a special visit with a friend, or the most wonderful make-believe story. Perhaps this is the first time that the child has voluntarily told you something. When this happens, use the Anecdotal Note form on page 27 to include in the child's record.

Social-Emotional Milestones for Three- to Four-Year-Olds

Every child has a different timeline for meeting the milestones listed below. Be sure to communicate to family members that all children grow and develop at different rates. Also, realize that children have unique ways of demonstrating certain behaviors. For example, how one child shows interest in a story may be very different from how another child shows interest.

- Plays in groups of two or three children; moves beyond playing next to others and fully acknowledges the presence of others

- Takes turns and shares toys with other children; behavior at home may be different from behavior at school, so if family members question a comment from you, share the specific observations you made

- Uses words to obtain needs and wants rather than hitting, pushing, or grabbing

- Accepts and responds to teacher's redirection readily

- Shows concern for other people and animals; because children have an instinctive concern for those that care for them, showing concern to people outside their normal circle is a good sign of emotional growth

- Separates easily from family members; this occurs at different times for children—while some children never have difficulty leaving their family members, other children may struggle with it for years

- Likes to engage in make-believe play, such as copying family members; pretending is a key activity for children; watch for times when play extends to include one or more children or when props are used

Social-Emotional Milestones for Four- to Five-Year-Olds

As with three- and four-year-old children, timelines for milestones are different for every four- to five-year-old child. It may depend on the stimulation that a child receives at home, his style of learning, and his level of confidence in his own abilities. As you observe children, take all of this into consideration as you draw conclusions and make choices about developmentally appropriate learning experiences.

- Willingly tries new tasks

- Plays complex and interactive group games

- Shares toys with playmates

- Shows self-control when angry or upset

- Completes projects started

- Enjoys pretend games

- Cannot always tell what is reality and what is fantasy

Playing with Others

Encouragement of imaginative play is needed in early childhood classrooms for young children to develop the skills of dramatic play that contribute to their self-regulation and cognitive, social, and emotional development. Children will try on new roles in the dramatic play center, explore the architect within themselves with the blocks, and take the lead role when showing a friend how to do something new.

The classroom is a safe place to try something new (sharing a book), to show off a perfected skill (dressing up), or to practice skills (building tall towers with blocks). Sometimes, you have a child with little or no experience playing with other children. As the teacher, you need to support children who want to play with others. For a quiet child or a child who has never been with other children, being part of a large group can be intimidating. This child needs you to show her how to enter a group in play or how to respond when someone wants to join her.

Being part of a group during work or play is important. Children see behaviors modeled, and they copy the appropriate movements, sounds, and expressions in other situations. They need to experience how others solve problems, handle difficult situations, and respond to fun and excitement.

Tips to Encourage Interactive Play

When you see a child in the class not involved in play, approach the child and model play with him. The child's nonverbal cues may lead you. For example, Nathan usually watches his friends play with the blocks, but he does not join in. Tell him, "Nathan, it looks like the other children are having fun with the blocks. Let's join them." Take Nathan to the block area and ask the others if the two of you may join in. Encourage the correct answer and have Nathan join you and the others in play. At the beginning, Nathan may not talk, but simply play with the others. Always include Nathan in your remarks to the group. By showing Nathan how to approach and enter play, you teach him how to manage this on his own.

Another way to encourage children to interact is to supervise learning centers. Children may go from center to center on a daily basis. Sometimes, decide who will be in the groups together. That way, you can group those children who have similar likes and dislikes. While they move from center to center, you can call attention to the group's interests. Perhaps, when the children have completed center time, you can challenge them to do something else together. Since they have worked successfully together already, they may be comfortable enough with each other to construct a fantastic block city, paint a mural, or play a game.

A music center provides a unique opportunity to encourage interaction. Divide children into "bands" and tell them that each band can make beautiful music together by playing instruments. This gives children an opportunity to work as one. To make beautiful music, they must decide to play fast or slow, loudly or softly, a familiar piece ("Twinkle, Twinkle, Little Star"), or a new creation.

Observation Report

Name of Child_____ Date_____ Time_____

Played with: _____

_____

Center of Activity: _____

_____

Observations:_____

_____

_____

_____

_____

_____

_____

_____

- -

Anecdotal Note

Name of Child_____ Date _____

Child told me: (write the conversation) _____

_____

_____

_____

_____

_____

_____

_____

_____

_____

_____

_____

_____

_____

Language Development

Imagine going to a place where you cannot understand what everyone is saying to you because they speak another language. Then, imagine studying their language for a while. This is what it is like for young learners. They are born not knowing the language, but after only a few short years know hundreds of words, as well as rules of grammar and syntax. Language skills can be broken down into sound articulation, length of sentences, listening, and reading and writing.

Articulation is how well a child pronounces words and sounds. Some sounds are easy to make, so they are mastered first. They are the sounds for **p**, **m**, **h**, and **w**. Others, such as **f**, **s**, and **z**, may develop later. Most digraphs (**ch**, **sh**, and **th**) develop last. When evaluating speech, ask yourself if a child speaks clearly enough for others to understand.

A three-year-old child may talk nonstop. At times, it will sound like babbling, but he is in fact practicing and mastering words. Three-year-olds like to ask what things are. They want to know the names of things to increase their vocabulary. The teacher can help by giving more information than the child asks for. For example, a child may point to a toy and say, "Bulldozer." You can reply, "Yes, a big, yellow bulldozer. Are you going to build a road with the bulldozer?" You have just modeled vocabulary and given the child information about the job of the bulldozer.

By the time a child is four, speech should be fairly clear. A four-year-old has a larger vocabulary and may tell long, involved stories. As long as the child is not monopolizing your attention, let him talk! A four-year-old is discovering the power of the spoken word. He likes the reaction that certain language brings.

As children master sounds, they will put them together to form words and then short sentences. The younger the child, the shorter the sentences. For example, a three-year-old may say, "Look, a dog." A four- or five-year-old may say, "Look, a big, brown dog with a wagging tail." An older child has had more practice with speech and thus will have a larger vocabulary and use more complex sentences.

To learn the language and all of the grammatical rules, a child also needs to hear the spoken language. What a child hears at home is the primary source of language rules; early childhood programs are secondary. So, family members pass their grammar skills on to their child. The pronouns *I*, *me*, *mine*, *you*, *he*, and *she* are tricky to learn. Depending on the tense and structure of the sentence, more than one pronoun can refer to one person. The best way to teach pronouns is through correct modeling. Time and practice will help children recognize patterns and rules. Prepositions can also be tricky.

Reading enhances language skills in many areas. Reading allows a child to hear the rhythm of the language and the inflection of the voice as the mood of the story changes, as well as words, sentences, and syntax. Reading also helps develop a child's attention span. There will be times when the class discovers a story that they want to hear over and over again. Continue to read the story every day if children show interest. They are discovering new words and sentence structures.

An older preschooler may see words on the pages of a book and realize that they are the words being spoken. With exposure to environmental print, on street signs for instance, he realizes that the shape of the word depends on the letters in the word. Then, the child breaks down the words into letters, and he sees the same letters in other words. The child has just begun a vital prereading skill.

Language Milestones for Three- to Four-Year-Olds

Remember that a child most often models the speech patterns of her family members or caregivers. As you observe and evaluate, make note of circumstances at home, such as non-English-speaking family members. Consider, too, that if a child is not progressing through the following milestones, she may have a physical challenge that needs to be addressed, such as a hearing loss.

- Speaks in short sentences, usually without a great deal of extra information such as adjectives

- Shows a longer attention span while listening to others

- Listens to others at circle time; not just the adult in charge, but to peers as well

- Understands the meaning of common prepositions such as *in*, *out*, *over*, and *under*

- Waits for a turn to speak in a group

Language Milestones for Four- to Five-Year-Olds

Four- and five-year-olds typically experience much more than three- and four-year-olds. They are socializing with more people—adults as well as children. They notice more about how people speak and take on similar voice tones and speech patterns as those around them. On average, they become more comfortable with what they have to say—and, therefore, say it.

- Uses sentences that are longer and more complex

- Can recall a story and supply details of the story—stories that have been read to her and stories that have actually happened

- Can tell about an object when asked

- Can answer the *W* questions (*who*, *what*, *where*, and *when*) about familiar stories and events

- Can follow three-step verbal directions

Talking in a Group

Children need time to talk and share their adventures in a group setting. At opening circle, set aside time for children to tell exciting news that they may have. Remind children to share only one thing. Some children have a lot of things to say. If you sense that a child needs to tell you more stories, ask her to remember them and tell you during free time.

Do not force children to speak in the group. As children become confident with their speech and comfortable with the group of friends, they begin to share stories. Encourage elaboration by asking an open-ended follow-up question. By reflecting and asking a follow-up question, you are showing the child that what he has to say is important.

Another way to encourage children to talk in a group setting is to have a show-and-tell time. Show-and-tell works best when you send home a special bag with a child the night before it is his turn. For a class of 15 three-year-olds, three bags works well. This means that you have three children doing show-and-tell each day. With four-year-old children, two bags will work best. The older children usually have more to say about their items. Set a limit for how many items you allow children to share each time. When the child reaches that number in his talk, he must stop. Send everything else back home without the child talking about them, simply suggesting that he bring the

items back the next time. Have extra bags available for children to carry their items home. It works well to have a laminated note attached to the inside of the bag with guidelines, number of items allowed, any restricted items (toy weapons), and particular items that you may be looking for. During show-and-tell, ask the child open-ended questions about what he is showing to draw out his language skills.

Use show-and-tell to practice specific letter sounds or other curriculum content. For example, specify that whatever items are brought to share must be round like a circle, must be red like an apple, or must have the *m* sound in its name. Have children give two or three clues that describe their first item to share.

Finger Plays and Silly Songs

Children love to say and perform finger plays over and over. The repetition of the words reinforces phonological and phonemic awareness. Finger plays and silly songs improve language development, just as reading (hearing) a story many times does. When finger plays have motions that require children's fingers to move independently, they are building small muscles in their hands. The rhymes in a silly song remind emergent readers that language is fun.

Finger Plays

Ten Fingers

I have ten little fingers, and they all belong to me. (*wiggle fingers in the air*)

I can do lots of things with them. Would you like to see?

I can open them wide, (*open hands and spread fingers*)

I can shut them tight, (*make fists*)

I can put them together, (*clap once*)

And I can put them out of sight. (*put hands behind back*)

I can put them way up high, (*put hands above head*)

I can put them way down low, (*hold hands low*)

And I can fold them together and keep them just so. (*fold hands in lap*)

Here Is a Bunny

Here is a bunny with ears so funny. (*hold up index and middle fingers on one hand*)

Here is his hole in the ground. (*make circle with fingers and thumb of other hand*)

When a noise he hears, he pricks up his ears (*put fingers together*)

And jumps in his hole in the ground. ("*ears" go into circle*)

Five Little Monkeys

Five little monkeys sitting in a tree, (*hold up five fingers*)

Teasing Mr. Alligator, "You can't catch me!" (*place hands by mouth to "yell"*)

Along came Mr. Alligator, (*make alligator by putting palms together*)

Quiet as can be, and he snaps (*clap hands*)

That monkey right out of the tree. (*repeat four, then three, and so on*)

Finger Plays and Silly Songs

Baby Bumblebee

(hold a "bee" in hands and swing in front of body)

I'm bringing home a baby bumblebee. Won't my mommy be so proud of me?

I'm bringing home a baby bumblebee. OW! He stung me.

(open hands and release)

I'm letting go of my baby bumblebee. Won't my mommy be so proud of me?

I'm letting go of my baby bumblebee. He is happy to be free! *(Wave good-bye)*

Little Green Frog

(squat down and put hands on floor between feet to be a "frog")

Ga-lump went the little green frog one day. *(jump when singing "ga-lump")*

Ga-lump went the little green frog.

Ga-lump went the little green frog one day, and his eyes went blink, blink, blink.

Gray Squirrel

(stand with elbows close to sides, bent up, with hands hanging down)

Gray squirrel, gray squirrel, *(bend and straighten knees with each word)*

Swish your bushy tail. *(wiggle backside)*

Gray squirrel, gray squirrel, *(bend and straighten knees with each word)*

Swish your bushy tail. *(wiggle again)*

Wrinkle up your funny nose, *(point to nose)*

Put a nut between your toes, *(put finger on floor between feet)*

Gray squirrel, gray squirrel, *(bend and straighten knees with each word)*

Swish your bushy tail. *(wiggle again)*

Language Evaluation Sheets

Use the form below when assessing the level or accuracy of speech for a student. Have a conversation with the child or listen to the child as he or she talks with a friend. As you hear the listed letter sounds, check them. Do this several times to ensure validity with an accurate sample.

Name _____ Date of Sample _____

Date of Birth _____ Current Age _____

p	m	h	w	n	b	k	d	g	t	y	f	ch	v	th	sh	j	zh	th	r	l	ng	s	z

Comments: _____

_____

_____

Name _____ Date of Sample _____

Date of Birth _____ Current Age _____

p	m	h	w	n	b	k	d	g	t	y	f	ch	v	th	sh	j	zh	th	r	l	ng	s	z

Comments: _____

_____

_____

Name _____ Date of Sample _____

Date of Birth _____ Current Age _____

p	m	h	w	n	b	k	d	g	t	y	f	ch	v	th	sh	j	zh	th	r	l	ng	s	z

Comments: _____

_____

_____

Cognitive Development

Children are like sponges; they are eager little learners soaking up information. They are ready to learn and eager to please you. Children learn and grow developmentally. During the toddler and preschool years, children gradually develop their mental representation capacities, reasoning and problem solving skills, attention, memory, language, and emerging math and reading skills. These processes take years to be well developed because a child's brain continues to mature and the child is continually exposed to new experiences. Young children have age-related and developmental limits in their cognitive capacities, but they also have enormous abilities to learn, think, reason, remember, and problem solve.

Preschool-aged children often have one-sided reasoning. Show a child two identical glasses of water. Confirm with the child that the glasses are the same and that they have the same amount of water in them. Now, show the child a glass that is taller and thinner than the others. Have the child watch you pour the water from the first glass into the tall glass. Ask if the same amount of water is in each glass. The child will tell you that the taller glass has more. It is bigger, so it must hold more; the line is higher, so it has more. You cannot easily convince him that the glasses hold the same amount of water. If you pour the water back into the original glass and again have two identical glasses, the child will be convinced that you just performed a magic trick. The brain has not yet developed to the stage where the child understands that the water maintains the same volume in both glasses. However, with a lot of opportunities to explore and learn, the child develops the ability to understand.

Research shows that the adult brain has 100 billion cells, the same number as that of a six-month fetus. The four-year-old brain has 400 billion cells (*Inside the Brain: Revolutionary Discoveries of How the Mind Works* by Ronald Kotulak, Andrews McMeel Publishing, 1997). The brain knows that it is producing more cells than it needs. But, just how many it will need depends on the amount of stimulation that the brain receives during these preschool years. Provide many activities to excite and stimulate children's brains; then, observe and note each child's specific growth and development.

Routine helps children gain a sense of how long they can explore an activity. They may challenge themselves more if they know that they have time, feel trusted, and know that they are not missing out on something else. The routine you set during the day also helps preschoolers become aware of time. "In five minutes, we will have snack. After snack, we get to sing," may be the familiar announcement on Mondays. Children gain a sense of five minutes and know to expect singing with the music teacher. Providing a routine also helps children learn the days of the week. They do not go to school every day, so children learn which days they do go to school. The ideas of yesterday, today, and tomorrow may not be mastered in preschool, but some children gain understanding with the help of a daily calendar activity.

Seemingly simple activities and concepts, such as these connected with teaching awareness of time, are ideal opportunities to observe and assess the cognitive development of children. Note whether they understand the passing of time on a larger scale, such as birthdays or seasons. Narrow that down to comprehending the days of the week and/or months of the year, as well as minutes and hours.

Children will be eager and ready to learn. They will be proud of their accomplishments. Challenge them with activities that they can relate to from everyday life. Later, you can introduce letter recognition and sounds, shape names, one-to-one correlations, colors, and counting. Children who are ready to learn will. The others will absorb information until they are ready to understand how to use the information correctly.

It will be up to you to decide what children know at the start of the year and where they need to be by the end of the year. This is especially important for children who are entering kindergarten the next fall. If you do not know what the schools in your area require of incoming kindergartners, you may want to research this. Most school administrators appreciate the fact that preschool teachers want to work with them. Use the kindergarten readiness checklist on page 60 as an assessment tool.

Remember, no matter how thorough you are with your observations, there will be times when family members doubt your assessment of their child. They will be convinced that their child knows the information you say the child does not. The "universality of knowledge" should be your answer. A child may be able to give information to a family member who is drilling him with flash cards, but until the child really owns the information, he will not be able to give you the same information and use it. Remember, you are the professional, but you also are a partner with family members.

Cognitive Milestones for Three- to Four-Year-Olds

Children enter the early childhood classroom at different stages of development. To help you make judgments about a child's development, it is important to know a little about the child. Gather as much information as you can about children and do not prejudge them. Sending home basic interest inventories or working on them with individual children is a great way to begin the process.

After you have sufficient background knowledge of the children, you can begin to assess their cognitive skills. The following are some basic cognitive milestones for children aged three to four.

- Identifies primary and other basic colors

- Identifies regular shapes such as triangle, circle, square, and rectangle

- Draws a recognizable person with three parts

- Sees only one side to a problem to be solved

- Completes a five- to seven-piece puzzle

- Rote counts to 10

- Understands "same" and "different" but cannot always explain why

- Understands "smaller" and "larger"

Cognitive Milestones for Four- to Five-Year-Olds

The information on page 38 holds true for the following milestones as well. As you progress through the program year, keep detailed notes on each child. Remember that many factors can have an effect on whether the child is successfully accomplishing the goals. These factors include family dynamics, economics of the family, peer pressure (even at this age), and lack of family involvement.

- In addition to the colors black and brown, knows the colors of the rainbow

- Identifies more than just the basic shapes

- Identifies some letters of the alphabet, in particular the letters in his or her name

- Uses one-to-one correspondence in counting objects to 10 and beyond

- Completes a seven- to ten-piece (or more) puzzle

- Recognizes and repeats simple patterns

- Understands "same" and "different" and can explain why

- Learns and plays simple card games and dominoes

Color and Shape Activities

The following activities and games, which can be used to reinforce colors and shapes, can be used with three- and four-year-old classes. When possible, use card stock or tagboard, then laminate before having the children handle the pieces.

Calendar

Sunday	Monday	Tuesday	Wednesday	Thursday	Friday	Saturday

Purchase or make two blank calendars, each a different color. Be sure that they include the days of the week. Trim one just above the written days and one square below the words. Choose seven colors and shapes (red squares, blue ovals, and so on) and cut two of each from colorful paper. Glue the first set of shapes to the cut calendar, one shape per day (the squares on Sunday, the ovals on Monday, etc.). Put hook-and-loop tape on the second set of shapes and on the individual days of the uncut calendar. After singing your calendar song and pointing to the day of the week as it is sung, have the children say what day it is. If it is Monday, ask your helper what the shape and color is on the Monday spot. Then, have the child find the matching shape and use the hook-and-loop tape to attach the shape to the correct day on the large calendar.

Fishing for Colors and Shapes

Using five colors of construction paper, cut two fish of each color. Draw a different shape on each color fish (two blue fish with squares, two red fish with circles). Glue one fish from each set to white index cards. Laminate the cards and the remaining fish. Put a paper clip on the nose of each fish and place them in your water table. To make a fishing pole, use a large paint stirring stick with nylon cord for the line. Attach a magnet to the end of the line to attract the paper clips. Have a child draw a card, tell you the color and shape, and fish out the matching color and shape.

 **(See page 2.)**

Heart Match

Using white card stock, cut out one heart for every two children in your class. With an uneven number of children, round up. On each heart, color or glue a shape, using a variety of colors. Laminate and cut the hearts in half. To play the game, mix up the heart halves. Give each child one half, telling her to hold it against her tummy so that she cannot see the shape. Play music and have the children dance around the room. When the music stops, they may look at their cards and find the matching halves of their hearts. Have the pairs tell you what they have. Then, gather the cards and play again.

Basic Math Skills Activities

Counting Counts

One-to-one counting, or counting meaningfully, can be practiced every day at calendar time. Using the calendar from the "Calendar" activity on page 40, allow a child or classroom helper to add a date number every day. Once the new number has been added, count from number one. At the beginning of the year, have the class count together. By late winter, the calendar helper should be ready to count for the class by herself.

Estimation

Use a large, clear plastic jar as an estimating jar. Each week, fill the jar with something that goes with the current instructional theme or something that is a special treat. Use dinosaur counters during dinosaur week, use teddy bears during bear week, or have children take turns filling the jar at home and bringing it back. If this is your choice, have a child pre-count the items at home with a family member. Have children guess how many items are in the jar. Write down the guesses. On the last day of the week, count or tell children how many items are in the jar. This activity works best if the jar is filled with larger items so that you can count as a class.

Number Recognition

To start number recognition practice, make a set of numbers with felt and glitter glue. Cut felt into 4" x 6" (10.2 cm x 15.2 cm) rectangles. Use the glitter glue to write a number and the corresponding number of dots on each felt piece. One to 10 works best to start. Put these numbers on a felt board. On the first day of a new theme, cut out a picture that gives a hint and hide it behind one of the numbers on the felt board. Have a child guess which number is hiding the hint. He may just point to a number and say, "Oh, this one? The straight line?" You might respond, "That's a one; is *one* your guess?" Then, look. If it is not right, accept more guesses until the hint is found.

Letter Recognition Activities

Nifty Names

Create name cards with children's names. Have each child look at her own name and spell it to you as she points to the letters. Children who complete the task too quickly should start over, pronouncing each letter distinctly. As children begin to recognize letters in their names, you will notice that they also recognize letters in their friends' names. Make a note of what you observe about lack of recognition or an advanced ability.

Match Game

Make an ABC matching game using the upper- and lowercase letters of the alphabet. There are many variations of this type of matching game. Teach letter recognition in incremental steps. Use cards showing pictures. Have children say the picture name when matching it to the letter sound. For example, if you showed a picture of a dog, a child would say, "dog, **d**." Another version of the game is to match the picture to the letter. Next, have matching card sets with just letters (all lowercase or all uppercase) and match upper- and lowercase together.

Letter Check

Use the cards from the matching game above and the checklist on page 43 to assess letter recognition. Have children name the letters, not just the sounds. Assess the letters that children can name and recheck periodically as needed. Keep the charts in children's files until full.

Another assessment for letter recognition is the chart on page 44. Circle the letters that children can identify. Send the chart home periodically so that family members can see a child's progress. Make a copy for yourself to use for comparison purposes at a later date.

Both checklists are organized randomly rather than in alphabetical order. This will allow children to use their alphabet knowledge, rather than location, to identify the letters.

Letter Recognition Checklist

Name: _____ Date: _____

DATE	Z	U	O	I	B	Y	T	N	H	A	S	M	G
DATE	F	C	J	P	V	D	K	Q	W	E	L	R	X
DATE	z	u	o	i	b	y	t	n	h	a	s	m	g
DATE	f	c	j	p	v	d	k	q	w	e	l	r	x

Letter Checklist for Home

Dear _____ :

_____ can identify the following circled letters.

Uppercase Letters

Z E G I O W X B A

R D S F T K J U P

H Q L C N Y M V

Lowercase Letters

l m f v n y q h d

s a r p u j t b k

c x o w i g e z

Cognitive Skills Assessment Chart: Three- to Four-Year-Olds

Date	Knows colors	Knows shapes	Draws person—3 parts	Completes 5–7 piece puzzle	Counts to _____					
Names										

✔ = yes, ✘ = no, put number child meaningfully counts to

Cognitive Skills Assessment Chart: Four- to Five-Year-Olds

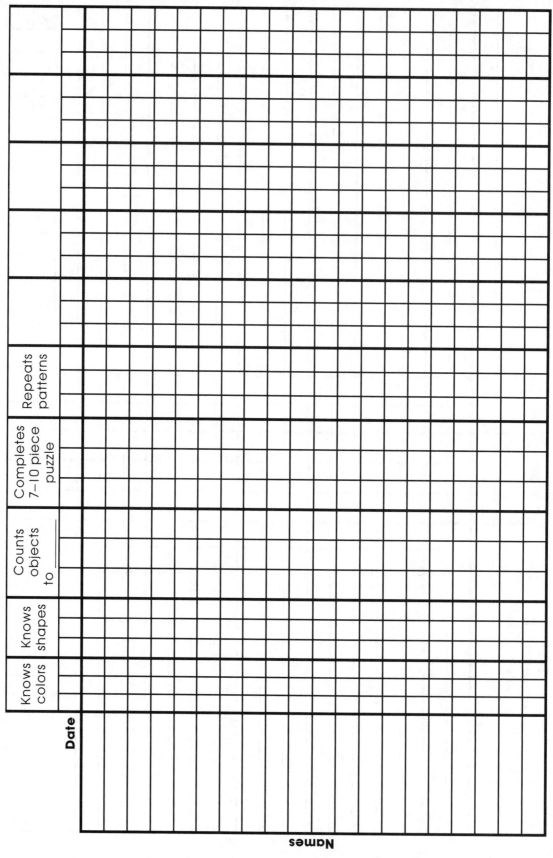

Knows colors | Knows shapes | Counts objects to ___ | Completes 7–10 piece puzzle | Repeats patterns

Date

Names

✔ = yes, ✘ = no, put number child meaningfully counts to

Physical Development

Physically, children develop from the trunk (or heart) out. Think of a newborn baby. She cannot even lift her head off her mother's shoulder. Think of the family members' excitement when they describe how she lifts her head off her mother's shoulder and looks around. This is the first step in physical development for the baby. By the time the child enters preschool, she will be walking, run-walking, throwing, and climbing. Those actions may still be awkward and will need more practice before they are mastered.

As a child gets older, the large muscle (or gross motor) movements become smoother and more controlled. The three-year-old usually "run-walks" when running and cannot always stop or turn as she would like to. By the time the child is four or five, she has a smooth run. She should be able to stop or turn quickly without losing her balance.

It is important to provide opportunities for children to practice these gross motor skills. More and more, elementary schools are filling their curriculums with academic activities and cutting out large muscle time. They are shortening recess times to accommodate the increased curriculum. The brain is set for optimum learning of physical skills during the preschool and early elementary years. Because elementary schools are shortening or eliminating these activities, gross motor movement becomes very important in the preschool classroom. As an early childhood educator, you must observe and assess the physical development of young children and help them develop the abilities.

Occasionally, you may have a child in the classroom who is considerably taller or larger than the other children. You may notice that this child lags behind in large motor skills or that he moves like a toddler or more awkwardly than other children. This usually means that the child's bones have grown quickly and the muscles have not had time to catch up. At parent-teacher conference time, show the family members the physical skills that are usually mastered by this point. Once the family members see the deficiency of skills, you may gently suggest an organized activity for this child to improve his skills. Good activities for this age are gymnastics, karate, swimming, and dance.

Gross Motor Skills

When planning gross motor activities, keep safety in mind. If the school has a gym, you may want to limit the number of children using the room at one time so that they do not bump into each other. You may need to set limits on climbing equipment such as how many children may be on top at one time or how they may slide down the slide. Usually, the skill level of the group or your own comfort level sets these limits. Inevitably, someone will get hurt. You may want to invest in a first aid course so that you can confidently handle bumps, bruises, and cuts.

Other hints to remember:

- The smaller the child is, the larger the ball should be. Large bouncy balls work best in preschool. A three-year-old will hold her arms stiffly to catch a ball. She can catch a large ball more easily by hugging it.

- Balance beams should be just a few inches off the floor. Children fall and slip a lot as they learn this skill. Short falls produce fewer tears.

- If you have scooter boards, remind children to ride these on their bellies or bottoms. When used as a skateboard, these become dangerous to the rider and other children.

On pages 49–50 is a list of activities to do in class to encourage gross motor development. You may want to copy the list of activities for family members to use at home. Include a small list of gross motor skills that children should master, such as walking up and down stairs, walking forward and backward, running, jumping in place, hopping on left and right feet, throwing a ball forward, galloping, and skipping.

 **(See page 2.)**

Gross Motor Skills Activities

Obstacle Course

Create an obstacle course in the classroom for children to go over, under, around, through, and on various objects (chairs, tables, beanbags, a mat, etc.). This develops planning and spatial awareness.

Rowboat

Have two children sit on the floor facing each other. They should hold hands, place feet together, and "row" back and forth. This develops body strength.

Bunny Hop

Have children hop beside a rope or tape line. This develops eye-foot coordination.

Slalom

Have children ride a scooter board or tricycle back and forth through obstacles. This develops eye-foot coordination.

Log Roll

Have children roll up and down a hill or across carpet. This builds body strength.

Pom-Pom Throw

Make pom-pom balls from yarn, place a basket on the floor, and have children throw the balls into the basket. This develops eye-hand coordination.

Popcorn

Have children pretend to be popping popcorn. They should squat down to the floor and "pop" up, repeating several times. This develops hip and leg strength.

Ice Skating

Have children put their feet on two pieces of paper or two wooden blocks. They should "skate" by sliding their feet across the floor. This develops eye-foot coordination.

Rescue Pull

Hold on to a rope and give the other end to a child who is sitting on a scooter board. The child should pull himself to you using a hand-over-hand motion. This develops upper body strength.

Gross Motor Skills Activities

Snake

Have children lie on the floor and wiggle and slither around on their tummies. Tell them to hiss like a snake. This develops body awareness.

Spider Web

Have children sit in a circle with their legs extended to their sides and feet touching the feet next to them. Tie the loose end of a yarn ball to a child's foot and roll the yarn ball to another child. This child should wrap yarn around one of her feet and roll the ball to someone else. Continue until all children have become part of the spider web. This develops eye-hand coordination.

Bear Walk

Have children bend over from the waist and touch the floor with their hands. Keeping their legs stiff and straight, they should move forward, walking the hands and plodding the feet. Tell them to keep their heads up and to growl like bears. This develops strength, coordination, and flexibility.

Crab Walk

Have children sit on the floor and place their hands on the floor behind them and their feet flat on the floor. Tell them to push up with their hands and feet so that their bottoms are off the floor and then crab walk across the room. This develops body strength.

Balloon Fun

Give each child a small, inflated balloon. Challenge children to bat the balloon in the air with their hands while moving from one end of the room to the other. Tell them to try not to let the balloons touch the floor. This develops eye-hand coordination.

 (See page 2.)

More Balloon Fun

Using the same balloons from the previous activity, have children hold a balloon between their knees and hop around a marked trail. This develops hip and leg muscles.

 (See page 2.)

Fine Motor Skills

Just as the large muscles need to grow and develop for children to master gross motor skills, the small muscles in the hands need to develop for fine motor skills. By the age of three, the small muscles in the hands have developed enough for a child to have some control when coloring and cutting. The child has also developed the patience and interest to practice these skills.

Drawing and writing are more complex skills than most people realize. Not only do the muscles in the hands need control, but also the muscles in the shoulders

and arms. The small muscles need strength for learning these skills. As you help a child hold a pencil or a pair of scissors correctly, you can feel whether the small muscles have any control or strength. Activities listed on page 52 help develop these muscles.

You will notice definite stages of development in a child's drawings. A three-year-old will grab a crayon and scribble. After filling a page, he will look at his creation and then tell you what the drawing is. As the three-year-old progresses, he will begin to copy shapes for you. Not until the age of four do you usually see recognizable shapes in a child's drawing.

No matter what age, some children do not want to stop moving their bodies. They do not want to leave play to practice fine motor skills.

Since these skills need just as much practice, it is up to you to entice children with activities that work on these skills. To encourage success, try the following:

1. Provide activities throughout the day.

2. Begin at the child's level; then, add a challenge.

3. Offer a variety of activities to interest the children.

4. Praise, praise, praise all honest attempts.

Fine Motor Skills Activities

Use any or all of these fine motor activities when assessing development. Make note of any progress. Indicate whether the strength is left- or right-handed or whether it changes.

- Have children squeeze, roll, and pull apart play dough to work the fine motor muscles. The fewer tools children use, such as cookie cutters and rolling pins, the more beneficial for the muscles. Observe how children use their hands and fingers to manipulate the dough.

- Have children use linking cubes or logs, making sure that they are snapping or linking the pieces correctly.

- Have children crumple scrap paper into balls and toss them into a basket.

- Ask children to use a turkey baster to blow cotton balls across a table.

- Have children string beads onto yarn or twine.

- Let children play with lacing or sewing cards using a shoelace as the plastic tip or a very dull needle tool. The cards can be purchased or easily made using stiff card stock and a hole punch.

- Ask children to tear paper using the thumb and index finger only.

- Invite children to wear fun plastic rings; then, have them tap their fingers to music.

- Teach and do finger plays during circle time and other times throughout the day.

- Let children glue small, safe objects onto paper to make a collage. Make sure that the children glue each piece individually instead of using a line of glue.

Pre-scissor Activities

Pre-scissor activities require a child to hold an object steadily with one hand while the other hand performs a motion. The thumb and index finger move in a pinching movement and involve the forearm or wrist in a turning motion. Have children complete the pre-scissor activities below.

- Using small plastic jars, screw the lids on and off of small plastic jars with one hand while the other hand firmly grasps the jar.

- Clip clothespins onto a paper plate while holding the plate with the other hand. Then, unclip and remove each clothespin.

- Move a boat across the water by squirting water from an empty dish soap bottle. Use only one hand to do the squirting.

- Hang a ball from the ceiling. Use the air in a turkey baster to swing the ball.

- Punch holes across an index card using a paper punch. Then, weave a shoelace or yarn through the holes.

- Using plastic scissors, cut play dough "snakes" into smaller pieces.

- Snip strips of construction paper ½" (1.3 cm) wide to make confetti.

- Cut out coupons from the coupon sections in the newspaper. Make a collage of favorite things.

Pencil and Scissor Grasps

Pencil Grasp

Children go through three distinct stages when mastering the correct pencil grasp:

Palmer Grasp

A child uses his entire hand to hold the pencil in the palm. There is no control when using the palmer grasp, and usually a child merely scribbles.

Four-Finger Grasp

A child holds the pencil with her thumb on one side of the pencil and her four fingers on the other side. The fingers are usually straight, and a child has some control when writing.

Correct Grasp

The index finger and thumb are on opposite sides "pinching" the pencil while the middle finger supports from behind. This allows the most control since the muscles are the most developed.

Scissor Grasp

Helping children learn how to use scissors need not be dangerous. Start with blunt safety scissors and remind children to cut only when the scissor blades are on paper.

Have each child place his thumb into the smaller hole and his forefinger and middle finger into the bigger hole. Some children gain stability by placing their ring fingers in the larger hole as well.

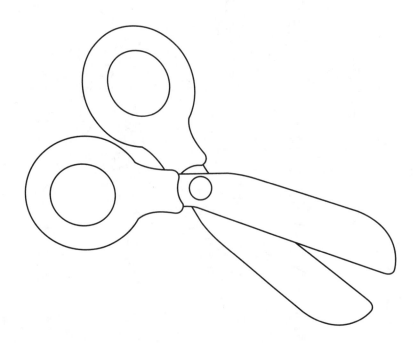

Physical Milestones for Three- to Four-Year-Olds

While every child develops at a different pace and to a different level, there are basic milestones or accomplishments that you can look for as reference points for development. As you observe children, take into consideration such factors as general health and physical development. Make note of anything significant that may or may not be affecting achievement of the milestones.

1. Uses fingers to pick up small objects such as coins, counters, and pasta

2. Builds a tower with a minimum of nine small cubes

3. Uses correct grasp when holding a pencil (after instruction)

4. Jumps in place on two feet

5. Balances on one foot for five seconds (note if the child alternates feet)

6. Bounces and catches a large ball

7. Throws a ball forward

8. Catches a lightly tossed or bounced ball with two hands

9. Uses an overhand climb when climbing on play equipment

Physical Milestones for Four- to Five-Year-Olds

As children get older, they should naturally continue developing physically. In your assessments, note any significant areas of delay or advancement. These notes can help you and the families track progress. They can also be used by family members to question their child's physician about significant delays that may be occurring. Remember that no one-time observation or assessment is enough to make a well-informed judgment. Use several different parameters before becoming too concerned.

1. Uses correct pencil grasp (after instruction)

2. Cuts with child-sized scissors (after instruction)

3. Copies simple shapes or patterns onto paper

4. Copies name

5. Throws a ball with some accuracy and catches a ball

6. Balances on one foot for minimum of 10 seconds and can alternate feet

7. Hops on one foot and can alternate feet

8. Gallops smoothly

9. Walks on a balance beam

10. Uses stairs for going up and down without support of a handrail

Fine Motor Assessment Chart: Three- to Five-Year-Olds

Date	Uses fingers to pick up small objects	Builds tower of 9 cubes	Pencil grasp	Draws simple shapes	Writes name	Scissor grasp				

Names

✔ = yes, ✘ = no; Pencil grasp: P = palmer, F = four finger, C = correct

Gross Motor Assessment Chart: Three- to Four-Year-Olds

Date	Jumps in place	Balances on one foot, 5 sec.	Bounces and catches ball	Throws ball	Catches ball 2 hands	Uses overhand climb				

Names

✔ = yes, ✗ = no

Gross Motor Assessment Chart: Four- to Five-Year-Olds

Date	Throws and catches ball	Balances on one foot, 10 sec.	Hops 5 times	Gallops smoothly	Walks balance beam	Climbs stairs; no support				

Names

✔ = yes, ✖ = no

Kindergarten Readiness Checklist

Name: _____ Birth Date: _____

Cognitive Skills

_____ Gives complete name

_____ Matches like colors

□ △ ○ ◇ ▭

_____ Names basic shapes (above)

_____ Counts _____ objects meaningfully

_____ Rote counts to _____

_____ 3 5 2 8 1 9 6 10 7 4
Identifies numerals (above)

_____ Makes size comparisons (big/little)

_____ identifies letters of first name

Language Skills

_____ Follows _____ directions

_____ Listens to a 5- to 10-minute story

_____ Obeys prepositional commands

_____ Demonstrates knowledge of first, middle, last

_____ Tells about an object or event upon request

_____ Asks and answers who, what, where, why, when questions

_____ Listens to classmates in circle time

Fine Motor Skills

_____ Cuts with scissors

_____ Grasps pencil correctly

_____ Copies simple shapes and patterns

_____ Draws a recognizable person

_____ Copies name

Gross Motor Skills

_____ Hops on one foot
_____ left _____ right

_____ Gallops smoothly

_____ Jumps on both feet

_____ Performs ball skills

_____ Balances on one foot

_____ Walks on a balance beam

Social Skills

_____ Plays interactive group games

_____ Shares toys with playmates

_____ Complies with reasonable requests from an adult

_____ Participates in group songs and finger plays

_____ Follows classroom rules

_____ Completes projects

As an early childhood professional, you begin every program year ready for the successes and challenges of a new group of children. This section of *Preschool ABC's* will assist in preparing children for a year of cooperative learning opportunities and relationship building. Developing good friendships and life skills will benefit children in future learning and in virtually all relationships throughout their lives.

The topics in the Behavior section of this book include *Discipline*, *Anger Management*, *Sharing*, *Patience*, and *Self-Regulation*. The Discipline section offers effective keys to creating a good plan for behavior management in the classroom. Activities, songs, checklists for tracking growth, letters home, and relevant reading lists for children are included in the next four sections. Be aware of teachable moments that give you opportunities to develop meaningful approaches. Involving children in choosing and developing activities gains their trust and builds their confidence.

The goal of the Behavior section of this book is to equip you with varied and flexible tools that can be implemented as each new and unique group of children enters the classroom. Through your intuitive use of the ideas presented, the class will find many solutions to common classroom challenges.

An emphasis on self-regulation is developed throughout the book. With that in mind, we must examine our own natural tendencies to react strongly when feeling upset. Be sure to react calmly and be in control during out-of-control circumstances. When dealing with a child who has lost self-control, please remember the following important factors. Losing self-control is a process. The earlier you can identify that composure is being lost, the more quickly self-control will be reestablished. Offer the child time-out. Use a soft and slow voice in communicating with the child. Respond to her in the method that works best for her. For example, proximity or distance can be an effective calming strategy. While a soft hand on a shoulder might be reassuring to one child, it might be highly threatening to another. Keep your gestures and eye contact relaxed and friendly. Count to 10, reminding yourself not to clench your jaw. Relax your visual gaze and rest your own arms or fists.

The words you choose during problem solving with a student are extremely important. Use encouraging words. Definitely avoid engaging in an argument. Arguing communicates a lack of control on your part and a window of opportunity for the problem to escalate. If you feel that you are losing your cool, excuse yourself for your own time-out. Do not ever leave the room, but perhaps sit on your reading chair or at your desk for a slow count to 10.

What you model to children communicates far more than what you say. They will watch closely and may test you to confirm that your appropriate responses are consistent.

The power of praise is enormous. Children who struggle emotionally need praise often and immediately. Focus your words on specific achievements and save praise for when it is authentically appropriate. At first, it may seem difficult to find opportunities to praise a child who struggles with issues of self-regulation, but specific words of encouragement will help the child grow. At first, a simple, "I like how you are sitting in your place" may be all that you can summon. Over time, you will find positive elements to build on.

Compliance is a difficult undertaking for some young learners. Developmentally, young children are egocentric in their very being. They would prefer to dance to their own rhythm. Some children are born with a personality that demonstrates quick and easy compliance. Other children have extreme difficulty with even the seemingly simple act of following through as an adult asks. There is much research and discussion as to the effect of nature versus nurture on this topic. The goal of this book is not to examine "why" but rather to offer positive outcomes in fostering appropriate behavior.

An effective method for developing compliance is to offer short and specific requests that can be followed easily. Allowing a young child to succeed with simple directions spirals him toward multi-leveled compliance later. Each child will present on a very different level on the continuum. Part of your responsibility as an early-childhood educator is to intuitively approach each child on his developmental level.

Enjoy! The goal is not to accomplish everything in this book. Rather, choose from year to year based on the emotional and social needs and the learning styles of children. Some years, you may be able to use this entire book collectively. Other years, you will need to focus on where children's needs direct you. Remember, teaching self-regulation will empower children! They will follow your lead in attitude and in action. But, perhaps most importantly, they need to know that you have joy in your profession. If you are enjoying teaching, they will enjoy learning!

The Key to Appropriate Behavior

The most effective solution to behavior problems in the classroom is undoubtedly a good plan for discipline and classroom management. When you and the children begin each day with a clear vision of acceptable behaviors, you will be well on your way to avoiding potentially disruptive behaviors. But, an effective strategy takes more than wishful thinking and good luck—it requires a well thought-out plan.

All children have basic emotional needs: to feel loved, secure, wanted, and valued. The purpose of discipline is to ensure the safety of all children and to encourage respect for others and for property. Insisting on good behavior shows that you care. The key to a successful discipline strategy is knowing how to combine these concepts.

The first thing to remember is that in addition to needs, early childhood educators and children have basic rights: to teach and to learn in an orderly environment, to expect good behavior, and to receive recognition for good behavior.

Second, behavior has a cause. When you can get to the root of what is driving the behavior, you can then begin to teach a child a better way.

Third, behavior is a matter of choice. Children can learn even at a very early age that they can take responsibility for their behaviors. All choices have consequences. You can choose your behavior, but you cannot choose the consequences. Whenever you can make discipline a part of natural consequences, you eliminate a potential argument. For example, when playing at the block center, a child has a choice of behaviors. She can play cooperatively by building with the blocks, or she can choose to hit other children with the blocks. The natural consequence of choosing inappropriate behavior in this situation is that the child is no longer allowed to play with the blocks. You are not taking the blocks away; the child has made her choice.

In order to create a well-behaved class, it is important to set the stage for success. Providing an atmosphere where children can and want to succeed creates more time for fun and learning. Educators can prepare children for success and ultimately avoid or minimize discipline problems by following a few simple guidelines.

- **Talk less.** Children need guidance that is simply stated.

- **Use visual cues and nonverbal body language to communicate.**

- **Address the situation, not the child.** Children need to know that even when they make mistakes, it does not make them "bad."

- **Be realistic in your expectations.** Requiring children to behave beyond their years is an exercise in futility.

- **Make sure that discipline is immediate.** Do not wait. If you wait too long, chances are that children will not even remember what they are being disciplined for.

- **Make sure that the punishment fits the action.** Do not exaggerate the situation and give the child an inappropriate punishment. Recognize that an hour in time-out will impress the child less than five minutes.

- **Keep your voice calm and firm.** Also, keep a calm but firm demeanor. It will help you make effective decisions.

- **Be confident and assertive.** Knowing that you mean what you say will help children feel secure.

- **Be positive.** Comment whenever you see a child doing something right.

- **Help form good habits.** Children need to be taught how to behave. Introduce your rules and expectations up front. This gives children a chance to succeed.

- **Do not shame or belittle.** Take a child aside whenever possible.

- **Help children see the cause and effect of behavior.** Knowing that it hurts when she hits her classmate will help a child make future compassionate choices.

- **Apologize honestly when you are in the wrong.** Even teachers make mistakes. Make sure that you let children know when you are sorry for inappropriate behavior.

- **Offer choices.** When a child feels that he has some control, he is going to be more rational about making good decisions.

- **Validate feelings, then let the child solve the problem.** Say, "I know that you're feeling angry. What can you do about it?" This not only tells him that you value him, but it also lets him develop self-regulation skills that will help him be more independent in the future.

- **Establish a separate area for discipline.** Choosing one spot and using it consistently will be a visual reminder to the children about consequences and making good choices.

- **Use pauses and voice variation for attention.**

- **Show enthusiasm for the curriculum and the children.** When you are excited and interested in what you are teaching and learning, children will be too.

- **Give warnings before terminating activities.** Having a few minutes of warning to wrap up playtime will keep cleanup meltdowns to a minimum.

Coping Tips

Here are some tips for coping on those days when even the best management plan goes awry:

- **Count to 10.**

- **Ask someone for a hug.**

- **Take a deep breath (or several).**

- **Assess the situation: How much does this really matter? Will this matter tomorrow or next year?**

- **Use family members as allies with challenging children.**

- **When you feel overly stressed, get help.**

- **Try to see the humor in it all. Someday you may write a best seller about all that you have experienced!**

Looking out for good behavior and rewarding it are important steps in a good discipline plan. Children, much like adults, are more likely to respond quickly and favorably when addressed positively. No one likes a nag, and you will not like being one. Here are some ideas to positively influence children and their behavior in class.

- **Hand out rewards.**

- **Try to catch children being "good" and then be generous with praise and rewards.** Acknowledge their efforts with praise, hand stamps, stickers, comments, certificates for appropriate behavior, treasure chest trinkets, and special privileges. These are all ways to affect behavior positively. Hand out tickets to children who share, play quietly, cooperate, follow directions, and so on. Tickets can be saved and accumulated for extra playtime or a choice of a special activity.

Sign Up for Good Behavior

Post a large chart labeled "superstars" in a conspicuous spot in the classroom. Whenever you see a child cooperating, cleaning up as directed, or following directions on the first request, have him sign the chart.

Praise Phrases

Give encouragement and quick recognition with these sample praise phrases.

- **That was a first-rate effort!**
- **Great job!**
- **Fantastic work!**
- **I knew you could do it!**
- **You make me smile!**
- **You're a star!**
- **You did it!**
- **Awesome!**
- **You're the best!**
- **I love how you did that!**
- **We're getting better all of the time!**

- **That's the way!**
- **Now you're talking!**
- **We couldn't have done this without you!**
- **You're a V.I.P. in our class!**
- **Nice!**
- **Yippie! You did it!**
- **Go, go, go, go, go!**
- **That's an outstanding effort!**
- **That's it!**

Do Say/Don't Say

One of the most important skills to learn as an early childhood professional is how to phrase command statements. If you feel like you are always saying, "Don't," here are some suggestions for how to say, "Do."

Don't Say:	**Do Say:**
"Stop hitting!" →	"We're all friends. Please keep your hands to yourself."
"Don't stand up during circle time." →	"Please sit on your bottom."
"Don't throw the books!" →	"Let's put these books away carefully."
"How many times do I have to ask you to clean up?" →	"Let's see how quickly we can clean up together."
"Don't color on the table!" →	"Markers and crayons are for paper only."
"Don't yell!" →	"Let's use our inside voices."
"Don't run!" →	"We use walking feet inside."
"Don't take his toy." →	"Let's find a toy that you can play with until it's your turn."
"Don't you remember how to line up?" →	"Remember, we always stand in a straight line."
"Don't touch." →	"This is for looking only. Please keep your hands in your lap."
"Don't talk to me that way!" →	"You need to use kind words when you speak to me."
"You are not playing nicely together." →	"How can we work together so that everyone has fun?"

blue

red

green

Time-Out and Other Discipline Alternatives

A Word About Time-Out

Time-out can be one of the most effective discipline tools, or one of the most detrimental. It all depends upon how you use time-out in your discipline strategy. First, time-out is intended to be exactly what it says—a time out. It gives children an opportunity to take a break, calm down, and regroup. Sometimes, it sounds like a punishment. But, behavior is all about causes and choices.

- **Do keep time-outs short—one minute for each year of age is a good guideline.**

- **Do let a child know what time-out is for and when she will have to "go to time-out" for misbehavior.**

- **Do talk about it. Let him know why he is having time-out before he sits down. Talk about better choices before he returns to play.**

The following are some alternatives to time-out:

- **Divert, distract, refocus.**

- **Redirect.**

- **Restate the rules.**

- **Offer very specific choices.**

- **Divide and conquer. Keep children who do not mix well apart, if possible.**

- **Ignore it. Sometimes, choosing NOT to notice a particular behavior is the best approach.**

- **Use a behavior management plan and chart. These work very well and can be carried through at home.**

Behavior Management Plan

A Behavior Management Plan is an effective tool for helping a child improve specific inappropriate behaviors. It is a plan in which the educator partners with a child's family to support positive growth. Feedback is specific and immediate, and a reward is often given. Often, a family will provide a tangible incentive, such as the reward of a small toy or a piece of candy, when the child is successful.

The Behavior Management Plan is designed as a temporary tool. Short and defined time frames are important. The goal is to help the child move from earning external prizes as rewards to developing improved and self-regulated behavior. An effective Behavior Management Plan gradually eliminates the "prize" because the positive behavior becomes internalized.

Providing honest feedback to families when difficult information must be shared may be uncomfortable, but, when handled with sensitivity, the child will grow. An effective method of sharing a difficult idea can be done through a technique called "sandwiching." Begin with an authentic compliment to the child. Next, state the area of concern in a neutral but specific manner. Finally, end your comments with positive encouragement.

Choosing specific and reachable goals is key. The form below is an example. You will need to decide which specific behaviors to focus on based on the individual child.

- -

Anger: Emotional Outbursts

Plan For Using an Inside Voice   Student Name: _____

_____   I was able to use an inside voice during circle time.

_____   I was able to use an inside voice during center time.

_____   I was able to use an inside voice while getting ready to go home.

I am proud of _____ because _____

_____

Teacher Signature: _____

Family Member Signature: _____

Family Member Response: _____

Behavior Management Chart—Flowerpot

Make several copies of the flower pattern on colorful paper. Set a specific goal, such as lining up quietly. Determine a number of times to work on the behavior and the incentive. Write this information where indicated on the flowerpot. Add a flower to the flowerpot for each time the child or group makes progress toward the goal. Create a "How Beautiful!" certificate for all of the behavior management participants.

Goal: _____

Flowers needed:
_____

Incentive:

How Beautiful!

collected ____ flowers

for _____

You're really growing now!

Sincerely,

Behavior Management Chart—Dinosaur

Make several copies of the dinosaur spike pattern on colorful paper. Set a specific goal, such as playing nicely with friends. Determine a number of times to work on the behavior and the incentive. Write this information where indicated on the dinosaur body. Each time the child or group makes progress toward the goal, add a spike to the back of the dinosaur. Create a "Delightful!" certificate for all of the behavior management participants.

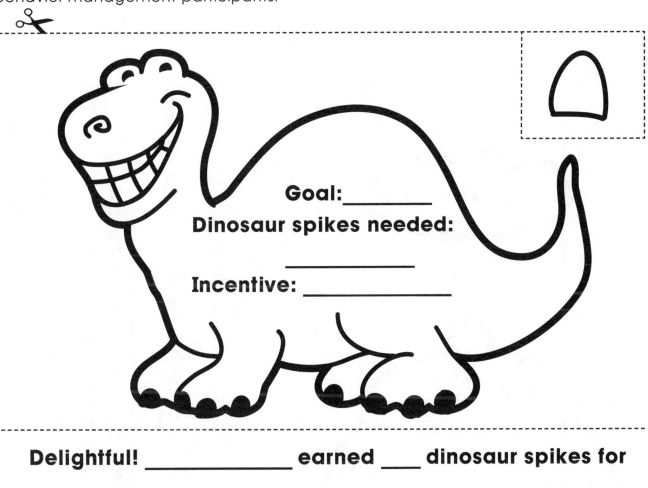

Goal:_____

Dinosaur spikes needed:

_____

Incentive: _____

Delightful! _____ **earned** _____ **dinosaur spikes for**

_____.

I'm so proud of you I could ROAR!

Sincerely,

Behavior Management Chart—Cookie Jar

Make several copies of the cookie and jar patterns on colorful paper. Set a specific goal, such as putting the blocks away without complaint. Determine a number of times to work on the behavior and the incentive. Write this information where indicated on the cookie jar. Each time the child or group makes progress toward the goal, add a cookie to the bowl. Create a "Yummy!" certificate for all of the behavior management participants.

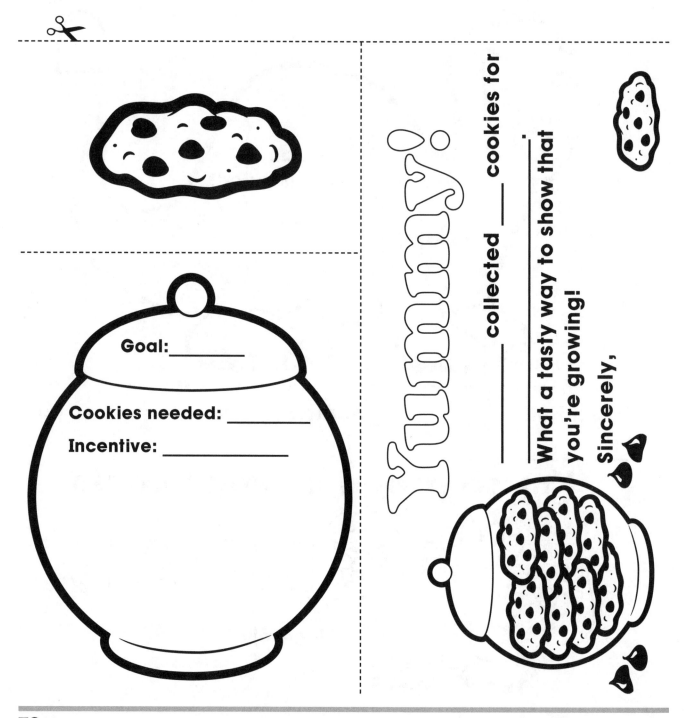

Goal: _____

Cookies needed: _____

Incentive: _____

Yummy!

_____ collected _____ cookies for _____.

What a tasty way to show that you're growing!

Sincerely,

Anger Management

Classroom Guidelines

Have children help brainstorm and establish classroom guidelines. Add picture cues to your words to help little ones remember. Post them in the room where they can be reviewed frequently. Do not forget to communicate with families in your newsletter or use the sample letter given on page 78.

Thinking Walk

To help children practice a strategy for calming down when feeling angry, lead them on a walk and model how they can "talk" to themselves through thinking. Line up in follow-the-leader format. Talk about how their hands may want to pound. Their feet may want to stomp. Their voices may want to shout. Explain how walking with self-control will help let all of those angry feelings slowly seep out and get smaller. When anger does not feel so big, it is easier to handle.

Volume Control

Children's voices are quick to reveal their emotional standing. Practice varying volume controls. Ask children to echo your words, tone, and volume. Begin with a whisper. Whisper a calm message like, "I am sharing my crayon." Slowly make your voice louder and louder. Children can also learn about volume with hand signals. Hold your hands beside your mouth to indicate loud or hold your finger to your lips to indicate whispering.

Thinking Things

There are many strategies for self-regulation that can be nurtured with little ones. Often, by distracting angry minds with smaller activities, emotions can simmer and emotional control and perspective can be regained. Share ideas with children. Add the ideas that they share with you to a list on chart paper.

Anger Ranger

Draw a person on an 11" x 14" (28 cm x 35.6 cm) sheet of paper. Explain how each child is like this person. Pretend that you are a child who says, "I don't like you." Put a single fold anywhere in the paper. Next, pretend that the paper is a child that you pushed out of the way. Put another fold in the paper. Open the paper back up. Show the children how all of those folds will never come out of the paper. Put-downs and pushing have the same effect. We feel better after an apology, but it does not completely take away what was said or done. Negative words and actions hurt.

Drawing Journals

Keep a quiet area in the classroom where children will each keep a journal of unlined paper for coloring and drawing. Ask them to show how they feel with colors or pictures. Since the fine motor skills of each child will vary, their response in their journals will vary as well. Begin the journals with positive feelings so that children develop confidence and a feeling of safety. Later, model in a journal of your own how you would color or draw your angry feelings.

Talk Table

Establish an area where children can discuss their differences with some guidelines. A small table with two chairs set aside is ideal. Model and role-play with children how to discuss a disagreement with a controlled voice. Honest feelings can be shared, but insults are not permitted. Fidget toys, stuffed animals, and paper for coloring can ease the tension for children attempting to work out differences while working at the Talk Table.

Peace Practices

Brainstorm methods for regaining composure when feeling angry, such as counting to 10, breathing deeply five times, running in place, wringing fists, or any other appropriate ideas that children share. Add illustrations to the list. Post them in the room where you can review them daily.

Songs to Share

My Mad Turns Glad

(Sing to the tune of "Skip to My Lou")

Mad, mad, I am so mad.
Glad, glad, I wish I were glad.
Mad, mad, please change to glad,
And turn around my day.

Blocks, blocks, I know I can share.
Cars, cars, we can work in a pair.
I can work it out with friends,
And turn around my day.

Glad, glad, it is a good day.
Mad, mad, it will not stay.
Glad, glad, no more mad.
I've turned around my day.

Think and Talk; Work it Out

(Sing to the tune of "Jingle Bells")

Think and talk; work it out.
We can get along.
Some days even when I'm mad
I'll keep my friendships strong.

Every day, I must play
With my friends at school.
Sometimes sharing can be hard,
But I will keep my cool.

Inside, outside, or at snack
Things may not go my way.
I can solve things peacefully
And chase my mad away.

Think and talk; work it out.
We can get along.
Some days even when I'm mad
I'll keep my friendships strong.

Songs to Share

Anger Away

(Sing to the tune of "Do You Know the Muffin Man?")

Anger, anger, is hanging around,
Hanging around . . . hanging around.
Anger, anger is hanging around.
Please, anger, go away.

If I could push my anger away,
Anger away, anger away.
If I could push my anger away,
Would my anger go?

Pushing anger won't make it go.
It won't go, no it won't go.
Pushing anger won't make it go.
It will only grow.

I will talk it out with you,
Talk it out, talk it out.
I will talk it out with you
Instead of pushing my anger.

I can draw in my journal,
In my journal, in my journal.
I can draw in my journal
Instead of pushing my anger.

Keep My Cool at School

(Sing to the tune of "You Are My Sunshine")

I get so angry, my face turns bright
   red.
You'd think I'm bursting with red hot
   flame.
But no, I keep cool.
I do not act out.
I keep my cool with friends at
   school.

My friend he pushed me. My friend
   she shoved me.
My friends were super-duper rude.
My teacher helped me
To make things better.
I keep my cool with friends at
   school.

She took my snack now. My lemon
   candies.
They are my favorite. A treat from
   Gramps.
My teacher helped me
To make things better.
I will keep my cool with friends at
   school.

Recommended Reading for Children: Anger Management

The following list is just a sampling of children's literature available. Add your own personal favorites to the suggestions below.

David Gets in Trouble by David Shannon (Blue Sky Press, 2002). The author/illustrator's connection with his readers is excellent. He even writes a short note to his readers to let them know that he had some behavioral struggles when he was little. Children are guided to take responsibility for their choices. Even wrong choices teach us important lessons.

Franklin's Bad Day by Paulette Bourgeois (Scholastic Paperbacks, 1997). The endearing Franklin actually has a very mad and bad day! He presents a stubborn attitude and refuses help from family members and friends. This is typical behavior for young children. Since children can already identify with the popular Franklin, they will be likely to identify with Franklin even in his negative choices. Finally, Franklin does work through his anger.

The Hat by Jan Brett (Putnam Juvenile, 1997). Lisa puts her hat on the line outside and the curious Hedgie ends up with it stuck on his head. The delightful exchange between the farmyard animals provides excellent examples of put-downs and buildups. Hedgie learns in the end that the one thing that made him most embarrassed was really something to be proud of all along.

I'm SO Mad by Robie Harris (Little, Brown Young Readers, 2005). Through the eyes of a child, a trip to the store causes a range of emotions.

I Was So Mad by Mercer Mayer (Random House Books for Yound Readers, 2000). Mercer Mayer's delightful creatures provide super character identification for little ones. The illustrations are just silly enough that a child will laugh at even the most aggravating ideas of anger. The gentle support of the mother throughout is powerful. The self-control and self-redirection at the end of the story provide a springboard for classroom discussion of finding solutions to problems.

Mean Soup by Betsy Everitt (Sandpiper, 1995). The explosive colors and rhythmic language in this story soften the tough ideas associated with anger. The simplicity of the book is powerful. The humor is effective. The solution presented at the end is developmentally appropriate and just plain fun. This delightful story can be turned into a super classroom activity. Allowing children to act out what is on the pages by bringing in their own "mean soup" ingredients will be sure to bring giggles and, even more importantly, foster the value of having a good sense of humor even in the most trying of times.

That's What a Friend Is by P. K. Hallinan (Ideals Publications, 2002). Establishing good friendship skills is a super way to ease children into more uncomfortable topics like anger. Remembering that we always have the support of our friends helps us work through both good and tough times.

Letter Home

Dear Families,

We have been sharing ideas for how to best handle circumstances that make us feel angry. Whether easily frustrated or not, at some point in time we all experience feelings of anger. It is important to know how to manage our anger. We also need to know how to respond appropriately when someone else is angry.

If we see specific concerns here at school, we will let you know. The design of our class discussions and of this communication is to be preventative and proactive in nature. By empowering children with knowledge about the emotion of anger, they will be less likely to act out in a physical way.

We used the following discussion questions to help us talk about situations that may arise at school. Please use these questions to talk about the importance of managing anger at home and at school.

What Would You Do If . . .

1. a class friend made an angry face at you?

2. a class friend pushed, kicked, or hit you?

3. you were getting so mad that you wanted to hit or throw something?

Would you rather . . .

1. be alone after behaving badly or talk to someone about it?

2. run around to get rid of your anger or color how angry you feel in a journal?

Enjoy this time together with your child. These young building years are important in establishing a lifetime of positive relationships!

Sincerely,

Anger Management Checklist

Name _____ Date _____

In class, we have been focusing on managing emotional outbursts of anger and responding to others who may be experiencing anger. Your child is now demonstrating the following:

> ✔ Indicates that your child is demonstrating consistently
>
> ■ Indicates that your child is showing progress
>
> ✗ Indicates that your child needs continued focus

_____ follows classroom guidelines

_____ asks for help when forgetting classroom guidelines

_____ asks for help when forgetting directions

_____ uses a soft inside voice

_____ uses kind words

_____ asks to share

_____ identifies positive emotion

_____ identifies negative emotion

_____ identifies when feeling angry

_____ asks for help when feeling angry

_____ identifies when another is angry

_____ initiates calm communication when another is angry

_____ shows respect to adults

_____ shows respect to other children

Child's Dictated Comments:

Teacher Comments:

Family Member Comments:

London Bridge

This classic activity is always a favorite. Sing the song "London Bridge" with the class, making sure that they know the rhyme. Have children take turns being part of the bridge until everyone has had a turn. When you are finished, have children sit in a circle. Ask questions to stimulate discussion about the game. What did they enjoy more, being the bridge or going under it? Why was it good to take turns being the bridge? Ask other questions that might help children see the importance of taking turns.

I Spy

For this activity, have children sit on the floor or at their desks or do whatever works best in the classroom. Tell them that they need to be very quiet and use only their eyes to look around the room. Model the game by doing the following. Say to children, "I spy with my two eyes something that we all can share." Then, begin to describe the item, one small clue at a time, until someone guesses what it is. (Suggested items: paint, sink, pencil sharpener, circle time rug, or classroom books)

Book Buddies

Divide the class into two groups. Have Group One children each choose a book to look at or read. The children from Group Two must then choose a "Book Buddy" from Group One to sit with so that they can read the book together. Repeat the activity so that the children in Group Two each choose a book, and the children in Group One choose a buddy. You may want to assist the children in choosing a buddy to help them make new friends. This activity can be extended into an art project in which children work together to create a picture that shows a scene or favorite character from the shared book.

Picture Pals

Have children work together in pairs or small groups. Give each group a large sheet of construction paper and a variety of items that they can glue or stick to the paper. Have each pair or group create a picture together. Make sure that children's names are on their pictures. When the pictures are finished, have a show-and-tell so that each group can share their picture with the other children. (Suggested items to have on hand: craft sticks, stickers, precut shapes, scraps of tissue paper, cotton balls, and star stickers)

Share-and-Tell

Replace show-and-tell with "share-and-tell." Have children bring an object from home that they can share with the class after they tell about it. Make sure that family members know that their child will be letting others play with her toy. You may want to do this activity over the course of several days rather than having all of the children share on the same day.

Lines and Circles

Have children form a line and hold hands. Ask them who is first and who is last. Now, have children form a circle. Have them hold hands again. Ask them who is first and who is last. Explain that when we have a friendship circle, no one is first and no one is last. We are all the same.

Always Room for More

Have at least half of the children sit on the floor in a circle where there is a lot of room. Have the other children stand outside the circle. Add children to the circle one at a time. Tell children to watch the circle grow and remind them that in a friendship circle there is always room for more. Talk about ways to change play to include more players.

Friendship Paper Chain

Cut strips of construction paper to make a paper chain. Have at least one strip per student. Before you interlock and glue the strips, make sure that each child has her name on a strip. Attach the ends of the paper chain so that the chain forms a circle. Hang the chain somewhere in the room so that the children can see it. Ask if they can tell where the chain link circle begins and ends.

Who Said Hello?

Have children sit quietly on the floor facing you. Choose one child to sit or stand next to you, facing the children. Have the child next to you cover his eyes. Then, point to one of the other children sitting on the floor. The child you point to will say, "Hello, Dustin" (use child's name). Have the child next to you open his eyes and try to guess who said hello. The children may use silly voices to try to trick the child who is guessing. This is a great activity for shy children and will usually quiet down the active ones.

Who's On My Right?

This is a great activity for teaching right and left. Have children sit or stand in a circle. Go around the circle and have each child say the name of the child on his or her right side. For example, Jamie would say, "José is on my right." Then, José would say, "Miranda is on my right." After each child has had a turn, repeat the activity by having each child tell who is on her left side. You may rearrange children and do this several times. It is a good activity for the beginning of the year when children are learning each other's names.

Songs to Share

I Can Share

(Sing to the tune of "Twinkle, Twinkle, Little Star")

It is always fun to share,
Showing others that I care.
I can share with girls and boys,
I can share my books and toys.
I can share my crayons too—
One for me and one for you!

I'm the leader, look and see,
Everyone will follow me.
But, when I am last in line
Everything will be just fine.
I can share by taking turns,
That is something I have learned.

This Is How We Learn to Share

(Sing to the tune of "Mary Had a Little Lamb")

This is how we learn to share,
Learn to share, learn to share.
This is how we learn to share
Every day at school.

We can share by taking turns,
Taking turns, taking turns.
We can share by taking turns
Every day at school.

We can share our favorite books
Favorite books, favorite books.
We can share our favorite books
Every day at school.

Add more verses with these ideas or let children create their own:

We can share our lunch or snack.
We can share our teacher's time.
We can share our crayons or glue.

We will share with our friends,
With our friends, with our friends.
We will share with our friends
Every day at school.

Songs to Share

Lots of Friends

(Sing to the tune of "This Old Man")

One and two,
Three and four,
Five and six friends, let's add more!
When we all play together,
We have a lot of fun.
Lots of friends are better than one.

Boys and girls,
Come along,
Let's hold hands and sing this song.
When we all play together,
We have a lot of fun.
Lots of friends are better than one.

I'm your friend,
You are mine.
How many more friends can we
    find?
When we all play together,
We have a lot of fun.
Lots of friends are better than one.

All Around the Circle

(Sing to the tune of "Pop Goes the Weasel")

(Have most of the children hold hands while standing in a circle. Have two or three children skip around the circle during the song. At the end of the song, they join the circle wherever they happen to be. Repeat using different children outside the circle.)

All around the circle we go
Trying to find a new friend.
'Round and 'round and 'round
    we go—
Hi, nice to meet you!

We Like Our Friends

(Sing to the tune of "Frère Jacques—Are You Sleeping?")

(Substitute names of children from the class.)

We like Keisha, we like Keisha,
Yes, we do, yes, we do.
Keisha is a good friend,
Keisha is a good friend.
Yes, she is; yes, she is.

Recommended Reading for Children: Sharing

The following list is just a sampling of children's literature available. Add your own personal favorites to the suggestions below.

A Chair for My Mother by Vera B. Williams (Greenwillow Books, 1984). A mother, daughter, and grandmother save coins in a jar until they have enough money to buy a chair that they can share.

Cracks in the Sidewalk by Crystal Bowman (Pleasant Word, 2008). A collection of humorous poems about everyday life. Contains poems about school and friends.

The Giving Tree by Shel Silverstein (HarperCollins, 1964). A beautiful story about a tree who wanted a boy to be happy.

Jared and the Ordinary, Handy-Dandy, Excellent, Extraordinary Plain Brown String: A Story About the Joy of Sharing by Dana Webb (Chariot Victor Publishing, 1999). Jared learns that there are many ways to share with others and discovers the joy of sharing.

Mail Harry to the Moon by Robie Harris (Little, Brown Books for Young Readers, 2008). The story of a young boy's acceptance of his baby brother.

Mine! Mine! Mine! by Shelly Becker (Sterling, 2006). When Gail's cousin Claire comes to town, Gail is asked to share her precious belongings. Illustrations convey Gail and Claire's feelings in an amazing way.

The Mitten by Jan Brett (Penguin Group USA, 1996). A boy loses his mitten in the snow, and it is shared by the animals.

The Rainbow Fish by Marcus Pfister (North-South Books, 1992). A beautiful but vain fish has no friends until he learns the importance of sharing.

Thidwick the Big-Hearted Moose by Dr. Seuss (Random House Books for Young Readers, 1948). Thidwick unselfishly shares his antlers with small creatures that need a home.

Letter Home

Dear Families,

Learning cooperative social skills is an important part of early childhood development. The classroom is a natural environment for young children to develop these skills. We are currently focusing on sharing and taking turns. The children are participating in group activities that allow them to interact and work together in positive ways. We are reading books and making pictures together. We are playing games, learning songs, and listening to stories that remind us of the many ways that we can share with each other.

Developing cooperative social skills equips a child to handle conflict as it arises. As children understand the importance of taking turns and sharing, they will progress from a "me-centered world" to an "others-centered world." Children will come to accept the fact that they will not always be the leader or the first in line. They will learn that sometimes it is their turn to talk and sometimes it is their turn to listen. As young children continue to develop socially, they will become more confident with themselves and their environment. They will have healthier and more meaningful relationships with other children.

We used the following discussion questions to help us talk about everyday issues that may occur. Please use these questions to talk about the importance of sharing and taking turns at home. Ask them why it is important and how they can share both at home and school.

What Would You Do If . . .

1. you wanted a turn to be the leader?

2. there were three friends and only two cookies?

3. someone wanted to play with your favorite toy?

4. someone was looking at a book and you wanted it?

5. someone forgot her item for show-and-tell?

6. your friend needed a yellow crayon?

Thank you for the opportunity to teach and nurture your child. Together we can make a difference in shaping young lives and helping them grow into responsible adults.

Sincerely,

Sharing And Taking Turns

Name _____

After our time of focusing on the importance of sharing with others and taking turns, your child demonstrates the following:

✔	Indicates that your child is demonstrating consistently
■	Indicates that your child is showing progress
✗	Indicates that your child needs continued focus

_____ lets others be first in line

_____ shares classroom materials with other children

_____ shares personal items with another child (when appropriate)

_____ listens while another child is talking

_____ plays cooperatively with other children

_____ takes turns during games or activities

_____ takes turns being a leader

_____ participates in class discussion about sharing

Child's Dictated Comments:

Teacher Comments:

Family Member Comments:

Patience

Manners, Please

Good manners and patience go hand in hand. Being polite takes extra thought, effort, and time. Besides saying "please," "thank you," and "you're welcome," encourage children to use each other's names. For a circle time activity, choose two children to demonstrate how to be polite. Give one child an object, such as a building block, and have the other child ask to use it, similar to the following example.

Darius: "May I please have the block, Julia?"

(Julia hands the block to Darius.)

Darius: "Thank you, Julia."

Julia: "You're welcome, Darius."

Don't Laugh!

This circle time activity will be great fun. Tell children to sit as quietly as they can. When you say "Go," they need to be perfectly quiet. Then, you, the teacher, need to make silly faces to try to get children to laugh. The first child to laugh is taken out of the game, but joins you in making silly faces for the next round. Repeat as often as desired.

Scribble Picture

Give each child a sheet of paper and a dark crayon. Have them scribble to create many shapes of different sizes. Next, have children use a variety of colors to color all of the shapes in their pictures. This is a simple, yet time-consuming activity that teaches patience.

How Long Is One Minute?

Help children understand the concept of time while involving them in a "patient" project. Give each child a crayon and a sheet of paper. Tell them to make small circles on their paper for one minute. You need to tell them when to start and when to stop. If the activity works well with children, try adding more time to the activity, or repeat using a different shape.

Fabulous Friday

Starting on Monday, and at the end of each day, praise children for something specific (for example, "You were good story time listeners today"). Tell them that they have earned a reward and place a handful of treats or stickers in a clear jar. Repeat each day, making sure that you have one reward per student by the end of the week. On Friday, when you praise the children again, pass out a reward to each child.

The Kindness Crowd

Have children sit in a group on the floor. Explain to children what the word *bully* means. Teach them the rule, "We're a kindness crowd—no bullies allowed!" After you have said it with them once or twice, just say, "We're a kindness crowd," and have them answer, "No bullies allowed!" Next, have the girls say, "We're a kindness crowd," and have the boys answer, "No bullies allowed!" Repeat by letting the boys start and the girls end. This will give confidence to children who are often bullied. It may also help the bullies make better choices.

Just Walk Away

When you are being teased by another, sometimes it is best to just walk away. You can communicate this message to children through this fun activity where they can pretend that they are animals (use appropriate motions):

Teacher: What would you do if you were being teased?

Children:
If I were a bird—I'd fly away.
If I were a rabbit—I'd hop away.
If I were a bug—I'd crawl away.
If I were a fish—I'd swim away.
But I'm a kid—so I'll walk away.

Sunshine Paper Plates

Give each child a white paper plate. Have him color the entire center of the plate yellow. He can also color some of the grooves on the outer edge of the plate to look like the rays of the sun. In the center of the sun, have him glue the following sentence (prepared in advance):

Kind words are like sunshine;

they make us feel happy inside!

We Like You Because . . .

This circle time activity will help children recognize the good in others while giving a boost to each child's self-esteem. One by one, have each child stand while other children say positive things about that child, such as, "We like Chandra because she shares her jump rope." "We like Sean because he makes us laugh." Try to avoid physical characteristics; instead, tell children to focus on their character qualities.

Songs to Share

Patience Please

(Sing to the tune of "There Was a Farmer Had a Dog—B-I-N-G-O")

Sometimes I have things to say
but if my teacher's talking,
I will raise my hand,
I will raise my hand,
I will raise my hand
Until she calls my name.

If I want to have a book
that someone else is using,
I will wait my turn,
I will wait my turn,
I will wait my turn
Until my friend is finished.

When it's time for all of our friends
to go outside to play,
I will wait in line,
I will wait in line,
I will wait in line
Until it's time to go.

Let's Be Patient

(Sing to the tune of "Frère Jacques—Are You Sleeping?")

Let's be patient, let's be patient,
Every day, every day.
There's no need to hurry,
There's no need to worry
When we work, when we play.
(repeat)

Be Polite

(Sing to the tune of "Do You Know the Muffin Man?")

It is right to be polite, to be polite, to be polite.

It is right to be polite, when we are at school.

Let's say thank you, let's say please, let's say please, let's say please.

Let's say thank you, let's say please, when we are at school.

Let's be kind and patient too, patient too, patient too.

Let's be kind and patient too, when we are at school.

Songs to Share

I Will Listen Well

(Sing to the tune of "Farmer in the Dell")

Oh, I will listen well, oh, I will listen
well.
I will listen with my ears,
Yes, I will listen well.

Oh, I will raise my hand, oh, I will
raise my hand.
When I want to talk in class,
I will raise my hand.

Oh, I will try my best, oh, I will try
my best.
Every day when I'm at school,
I will try my best.

Take it Slow!

(Clap and Rap)

When I get mixed up and I don't
know where to go
What should I do?
TAKE IT SLOW!

When I'm movin' too fast and
I go-go-go,
What should I do?
TAKE IT SLOW!

When I feel like runnin' 'cause it's
time to go,
What should I do?
TAKE IT SLOW!

Take it slow! Take it slow! Take it
slow! *(whisper)*

I Feel Like Moving

(Sing to the tune of "Skip to My Lou")

Wiggle my toes and wiggle my nose.
Wiggle my toes and wiggle my nose.
Wiggle my toes and wiggle my nose,
When I feel like moving.

Tap my finger on my knee.
Tap my finger on my knee.
Tap my finger on my knee,
When I feel like moving.

Teacher says it's time to march.
Teacher says it's time to march.
Teacher says it's time to march,
Now, I'm REALLY moving!

Recommended Reading for Children: Patience

The following list is just a sampling of children's literature available. Add your own personal favorites to the suggestions below.

Auntee Edna by Ethel Footman Smothers (Eerdmans Books for Young Readers, 2003). A young girl thinks that she will be bored at her aunt's house, but she finds new ways to have fun.

Be Patient, Pooh! by Kathleen Weidner Zoehfeld (Disney Press, 2000). Waiting is hard for Winnie the Pooh, especially when waiting for his birthday party.

Before I Go to Sleep by Thomas Hood (HarperCollins, 1999). Before falling asleep, a young boy imagines what he would do if he were different kinds of animals.

The Carrot Seed by Ruth Krauss (HarperCollins, 2004). A little boy plants a carrot seed and waits patiently while everyone says, "It won't come up."

Frog and Toad All Year by Arnold Lobel (HarperCollins, 1984). This book contains several stories about the friendship and patience of two good friends.

Leo the Late Bloomer by Robert Kraus (HarperCollins, 1994). A tiger cub eventually learns to read, write, and draw.

Maybe a Bear Ate It! by Robie Harris (Orchard Books, 2008). An endearing creature loses his favorite bedtime book and cannot sleep without it.

Patient Rosie by Mary Morgan (Hyperion Books for Children, 2000). A little mouse learns to wait for cookies to cool and seeds to grow.

Sheep, Sheep, Sheep, Help Me Fall Asleep by Arlene Alda (Yearling, 1995). Counting animals doing silly things can keep a child entertained (a rhyming counting book).

Waiting for the Whales by Sheryl McFarlane (Orca Book Publishers, 2002). A little girl watches for whales with her grandfather every summer evening.

The Waiting Place by Marc Sutherland (Diane Publishing Company, 1998). A sleepless child uses his imagination to entertain him during the night.

Winnie-the-Pooh Meets Gopher by A. A. Milne (Golden Press, 1978). Pooh gets stuck in Rabbit's hole after eating too much and has to wait until he is thin enough to get out.

Letter Home

Dear Families,

Being patient is difficult for young children, especially when their needs seem so important and immediate to them. Learning to be patient is part of developing good social and learning skills in the classroom. We are currently working on the emotional behaviors of patience, such as listening and being polite. We are practicing our manners in the classroom, and I encourage you to practice them at home. Saying "please," "thank you," and "you're welcome" takes a little extra thought and effort, but it teaches patience, as well as polite conversation.

Your children have participated in creative activities that require patience and focus. Ask them to show you their one-minute circle pictures and see how many circles they can draw. As your children grow in their ability to be patient, they will become better listeners and better learners.

We used the following discussion questions to help us talk about situations that may arise at school. Please use these questions to talk about the importance of being patient and being a good listener at home and at school.

What Would You Do If . . .

1. the teacher started reading a story that you already knew?

2. someone started talking aloud during story time?

3. you wanted to say something when the teacher was talking?

4. one of your friends whispered to you when you were supposed to be listening?

5. you wanted to go out to play but the teacher told you to wait?

6. you thought that story time was too long?

Thank you for the opportunity to teach your child. Together, we can equip them with the necessary skills to have a positive experience at school.

Sincerely,

Patience Checklist

Name _____

After our time of focusing on the importance of being patient, polite, and a good listener, your child demonstrates the following:

✔ Indicates that your child is demonstrating consistently	
■ Indicates that your child is showing progress	
✘ Indicates that your child needs continued focus	

_____ listens while the teacher is talking

_____ listens while another child is talking

_____ sits quietly during story time

_____ says "please" and "thank you"

_____ waits patiently in line before going out for recess

_____ waits to ask a question until acknowledged by the teacher

_____ listens to instructions

_____ follows instructions

_____ completes activities

Child's Dictated Comments:

Teacher Comments:

Family Member Comments:

Texture Play

One of the systems of the body that provides information about the environment is the tactile system. The tactile system alerts people about changes to protect them and to help them discriminate differences such as hard, soft, wet, dry, bumpy, or smooth. Many children who are beginning to develop self-regulation skills benefit from extra experiences with their tactile systems. Some simple tactile materials that can be incorporated into the classroom day are play dough (recipes on page 95), finger paints, shaving cream, pudding, sand, and water (add bubbles for extra texture and interest).

 **(See page 2.)**

Texture Seats and Games

Vary the texture of where children sit to stimulate the tactile system. Let children sit on beach towels, blankets, rugs, and foam of different thicknesses. Children can work with manipulative items such as puzzles or blocks. You may encourage restless children to work with partners playing tactile games like thumb wrestling. Or, class-size games can be played, such as "Duck, Duck, Goose" or "Hot Potato."

Lotion Potion

After children wash their hands, allow them to rub a textured or scented lotion into their hands. Powder, lotions, and antibacterial liquids can be rubbed not only into hands but also into arms, feet, and the lower area of children's legs. Use washcloths, towels, bath mitts, loofah sponges, or other textures to rub these areas of the body as well. Children will giggle as they are growing in ways they are not even aware of. Providing these types of tactile experiences is a proactive approach to impulsivity.

 **(See page 2.)**

Back Drawing

Have children work with partners to draw shapes or pictures with their fingers on each other's backs. Model, as children watch you, how to "draw" on one child's back. Show them how to "erase" a picture by rubbing gently over the entire back with a wide palm.

Tactile Recipes

Ask families to make these recipes at home or donate some or all of the ingredients. Copy the recipes below and send them home inside gallon-sized resealable plastic bags. Families can return the tactile products to school in the bags. Keep the bags at school for lots of tactile fun.

Play Dough

Mix:

> 5 cups (1.2 L) flour
>
> 1 cup (237 mL) salt
>
> 5 tbsp. (74 mL) of alum or cream of tartar (found with spices in a grocery store)
>
> 3 packs powdered drink mix (to give color and scent)

Add:

> 4 cups (0.95 L) boiling hot water
>
> 1/2 cup (118 mL) vegetable oil

Pour the boiling water and oil into the dry mixture and stir until blended. Let cool for about 15 minutes. Once cooled, knead until well mixed.

Squishy Putty

Stir together:

> 1 cup (237 mL) white school glue
>
> 1 cup (237 mL) water with colored food coloring

Dissolve:

> 2 tbsp. (30 mL) borax (found in laundry aisle) into 1 pint warm water

While stirring slowly add borax solution into the glue/water mixture. Knead. Mixture keeps well in the refrigerator.

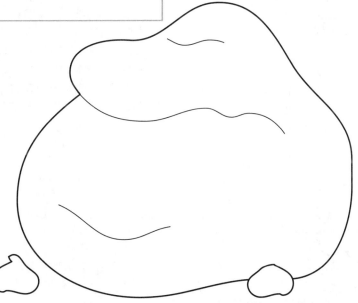

 **(See page 2.)**

Songs to Share

Wiggle and Jiggle

(Sing to the tune of "Hickory Dickory Dock")

I wiggle and jiggle around.
I skooch up and then I sit down.
I move over here. I move over there.
I wiggle and jiggle around.

I try and I try to be still.
I don't think it'll happen until
I breathe deeply in, and then I begin
To slow down my motor and chill.

I wiggle and jiggle around.
Outside where it's okay to be found,
Wiggling here, wiggling there.
I wiggle and jiggle around.

My Motor

(Sing to the tune of "Old MacDonald Had a Farm")

My motor runs so very slow.
How does my motor go?
I'm sitting still. I am polite.
How does my motor go?
I am relaxed here. I am relaxed there.
I am relaxed here and everywhere I go.
My motor runs so very slow.
How does my motor go?

My motor runs like a zooming car.
How does my motor go?
I'm speeding fast with running feet.
How does my motor go?
I'm grabbing here. I hurry there.
I am speeding here and everywhere I go.
My motor runs like a zooming car.
How does my motor go?

I am the key to my motor.
How does my motor go?
I can slow or speed it up.
How does my motor go?
I make a choice here. I make a choice there. I make a choice here and everywhere I go.
I am the key to my motor.
How does my motor go?

Songs to Share

Feeling Strong

(Sing to the tune of "Old MacDonald Had a Farm")

I'm feeling strong and tough and mad. But, I will have control.
I want to push or yell or run. But, I will have control.
Thinking first here, thinking first there, thinking, thinking everywhere!
I can control my impulses, I think before I act.

I'm feeling bossy, mean, and sad. But, I will have control.
I want to kick and pinch or nudge. But, I will have control.
Thinking first here, thinking first there, thinking, thinking, everywhere!
I can control my impulses, I think before I act.

Impulse Chant

(clap, pat, or snap to the rhythm while reciting this chant)

Impulse, impulse, impulse control
Means my actions I can control.
I may want to move,
I may want to yell.
But, I will control myself today.

Impulse, impulse, impulse control
Means my actions I can control.

Blowing Off Steam

(Sing to the tune of "Wheels on the Bus")

To blow off steam I can run a lap, run a lap, run a lap.
To blow off steam I can run a lap, all around outside.

To blow off steam I can shake my pillow, shake my pillow, shake my pillow.
To blow off steam I can shake my pillow, all around inside.

To blow off steam I can play the drum, very loud, very strong.
To blow off steam I can play the drum with big and strong feelings.

To blow off steam I can write or draw, write or draw, write or draw.
To blow off steam I can write or draw and let those feelings go.

To blow off steam I must stay safe, must stay safe, must stay safe.
To blow off steam I must stay safe so no one will get hurt.

To blow off steam I can have control, have control, have control.
To blow off steam I will make good choices and blow my steam away.

Recommended Reading for Children: Self-Regulation

The following list is just a sampling of children's literature available. Add your own personal favorites to the suggestions below.

Clifford's Tricks by Norman Bridwell (Cartwheel, 1980). Clifford has been with us for many years, but his love and his lessons are as timely today as they were long ago. Clifford learns how negative his fun-loving tricks are in maintaining friendships. Little ones often think that playing tricks is funny without thinking through the consequences.

The Dog Who Cried "Woof!" adapted by Bob Barkly (Cartwheel, 2001). Some lessons are timeless. The loving Clifford makes the mistake of "crying wolf," as most young children do. Children will learn the benefits of controlling the impulse to exaggerate and to seek help when it is not entirely needed.

Feet Are Not for Kicking by Elizabeth Verdick and Marieka Heinlen (Free Spirit Publishing, 2004). An adventure with feet—walking, standing, leaping, kicking balls and leaves—but not people!

Fred Stays with Me! by Nancy Coffelt (Little, Brown Books for Young Readers, 2007). A girl and her pet get into trouble at each of her parents' homes where she splits her time.

I Can't Wait by Elizabeth Crary (Parenting Press, 1996). A little boy has to wait for his turn, and he ponders how to handle this tough and common childhood dilemma. Children are prompted to consider many alternatives as the reading adult shares them.

The Way I Feel by Janan Cain (Parenting Press, 2000). This book can be a terrific discussion tool in helping children identify their feelings and make appropriate choices.

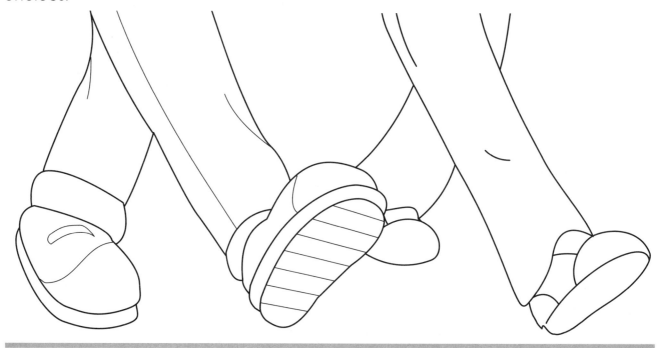

Letter Home

Dear Families,

Thank you for sharing your wonderful children with my class this year. It is amazing to see the unique gifts that each child brings.

Children come to school with various backgrounds, interests, and abilities. We try to cultivate the strengths of each child and build each other up as a community of learners. One of the skills necessary for children to work with others is the sense of being able to control natural impulses. For example, a young child's impulse is to call out information that she knows. In school, children learn to control that impulse by raising their hands and waiting for their turns to share.

There are many physical and emotional abilities that must be mastered before a child is able to self-regulate. In its very basic form, we explain to children that they can control their own "motor." They can practice controlling if their bodies are moving slowly or speeding very quickly. Some children understand this best when comparing their body "motors" to a vehicle with an engine, such as a train or car.

We have been working on paying attention to our bodies. We think about what our hands, feet, and bodies are doing. Are they in our own space or are they in another's? Are they helping us complete constructive goals, or are they keeping us from doing so?

Any conversation and activities that you have at home that support ours will help your child find success. There are many things that you can do to help your child, such as letting him play with play dough, "drawing" on each other's backs, or rocking in a chair together as you read aloud.

Thank you for helping your child build a wonderfully strong foundation so that all future learning will spiral toward success. You are the best gift and advocate that your child has. Thank you for all that you do.

Growing together,

Self-Regulation Checklist

Name _____

After focusing on managing our impulses and responding to others' impulsivity, your child demonstrates the following:

✔	Indicates that your child is demonstrating consistently
■	Indicates that your child is showing progress
✗	Indicates that your child needs continued focus

_____ sits with feet in own space

_____ sits with hands in own space

_____ sits with body in own space

_____ raises hand when wanting to share

_____ actively listens to adults

_____ actively listens to peers

_____ verbalizes when help is needed to gain better impulse control

_____ gives others their personal space

_____ stands in line with hands in own space

_____ walks in line with steady walking feet

_____ uses a quiet inside voice

_____ uses an appropriate outside voice

_____ uses an appropriate voice in solving conflict

_____ uses good-manners words

Child's Dictated Comments:

Teacher Comments:

Family Member Comments:

Strategies for Success

Before the program year begins, having an effective classroom management strategy will help set your class up for success.

Room Arrangements

Take a look at how you have your classroom arranged. You might find that you can control some of the behavior in your class by rearranging furniture. If there are shelves of manipulatives and supplies facing or surrounding the area where you sit for circle time or story time, children are quite naturally going to be interested in what is on the shelves. Arrange your room so that the manipulatives, books, and supplies are located out of sight of where you will be conducting circle time.

If you want the blocks to stay in a certain area of the room and not get mixed up with the crayons, create a labeled place for everything in your room, and create smaller spaces for each activity center.

Seat children who have a difficult time paying attention either next to children who have strengths in this area or within your arm's reach so that you can gently redirect them. And remember, being able to choose a partner in an activity is a great motivator for good behavior.

Activity Ratios

Limiting each activity or center to two or three children at a time will eliminate difficulties that arise when there are too many children and too few pieces to play with. Keep the learning centers varied, and change them often.

Awareness

Being aware and knowing what is going on in the room at all times is key to helping children keep within the boundaries that you have set in your classroom. Walking around and interacting briefly with each child will help you stop unwanted behavior long before it becomes a problem.

Pacing

Knowing when to move faster, slower, or onward is a key skill to master. When children are bored, they will often find other things to occupy their time. Keeping the pace where children have enough time to complete their play but not so long that they lose interest takes practice and sensitivity.

Above all, be aware of what is going on in your room at all times. Be flexible enough so that you can change the momentum quickly if things begin to get out of hand. Having a good classroom management strategy is important so that the children in your class can choose appropriate behaviors.

Setting Clear Limits and Expectations

Limits and expectations are how you let the children in your class know what is acceptable behavior and what is not. Limits are guidelines as to what is not acceptable. While setting limits may seem restrictive, children actually crave them. They like the security of knowing how far they can push and when you will push back. Children like limits because limits help them know what they can control. Having too many things to control is an overwhelming thought to young children. They often respond by being out of control when they have more choices than they can handle.

When you give your class clear expectations, you are letting them know exactly what is acceptable. Expectations tell them what they can do as opposed to what they cannot. Comments such as, "I expect you to stay seated during circle time" and "We cooperate and share when we play," tell children exactly what you expect. Children are eager to please, and knowing what you expect of them makes them work harder to stay in line than they would otherwise.

- **Do not assume that children know what to do.** Create the rules that you are going to have in your classroom together. (See Classroom Rules, pages 108–110, for suggestions.) Having a say in what the rules and consequences are may help children follow the rules better. Be firm and consistent in standing by the rules that you set together.

- **Keep it simple.** When setting rules, make as few as possible, and make them simple. Recognize that children's conflicts and misbehavior can be learning opportunities. When a child has multiple behavior issues, start with the most disruptive or unsafe behavior. Then, work your way backward to better behavior as new skills are mastered. Getting bothered about every rule infraction will leave you tired, frustrated, and wondering why you signed up for this job in the first place.

- **Be realistic.** It is not appropriate to ask small children to sit for long periods of time or to expect perfect behavior. In setting your expectations too high, you will be setting yourself up for disappointment and the children for frustration. A good rule is to have a child sit in a quiet place for one minute per year of age. Two minutes is a long time for a two-year-old!

- **Limits and rules must be clear.** "Get in line" is a command often given to children without thinking about the children's perspective. What is clear to you may not be clear to them. What does "Get in line" mean? Does it mean to squeeze between two other children? Does it mean to stand in a big clump at the door?

Setting limits that are clear will let children know exactly what to do, what not to do, and what the consequences are when they choose otherwise.

Modeling

Now that you have established limits and rules for the children in your class to follow, the next important step is to model your expectations. You know from watching children play that they frequently imitate the adults around them. After all, that is the business of play. What they see you or other adults doing is fair game when it comes to behavior. If they see or hear you rant or raise your voice when you are frustrated, they are likely to feel that it is fine for them too. If you fail to clean up the messes that you make in the classroom, they are less likely to see the importance of cleaning up after themselves.

- **Keep your message consistent by always following the same set of rules that you require of the children.** Not only will you be modeling good behavior, but you will also be sending a message that you mean what you say, and that you respect them too.

- **Role-play rules and demonstrate activities.** As you acquaint children with new rules, role-play with them to model appropriate and inappropriate behavior. Show them how to use equipment or centers and the rules or limits in each area. Place the children in small groups to act out or role-play different scenarios and appropriate solutions to situations, such as what to do when someone is hurtful. When you can make a spoken rule come to life, you will be reinforcing the learning and making it more meaningful.

- **Use other children as examples.** Using individual children who are on task and behaving as they should is a useful tool for modeling behavior in the classroom. A statement, such as, "I like the way Stuart is keeping all of the sand inside the sand table," helps show the other children what they need to do.

- **Validate their feelings and let them solve their own problems.** Much like children need to be taught how to read or tie their shoes, they need help in forming good habits. Saying, "I can see that you're angry. What can you do about it?" not only validates her feelings, but helps her know that she can do it all by herself. Giving her choices or recommendations will be helpful to her in forming a good plan.

- **Help children learn the value of cause and effect.** Helping children see the cause and effect of their behavior will help them make better choices. In the egocentric world of young children, thinking about how another child feels is a new and complicated concept.

Routines and Consistency

Routines and consistency are important in young children's lives. Having a specific order for events, specific places for manipulatives and supplies, and specific rules that do not change give children security and continuity. So, how do you establish routines and consistency?

- **Say what you mean and then do it.** If you tell a child that he will have to stop coloring if he continues to break the crayons, you need to follow through and remove him immediately if he continues to do what you asked him not to do. He will know that you mean business, and he will be more likely to respond quickly next time. When you continue to warn, cajole, or threaten and then do not follow through, he will know that not only are you not going to stop him from breaking crayons, you probably will not discipline him for other poor choices either. Knowing that you will do what you say every time sets you up for future success with the children.

- **Do not make promises you cannot or do not intend to keep.** If you promise a certain reward for good behavior, be sure to follow through. Children have incredible memories for some details, and this is one of them. Do not threaten something that you cannot follow through with. For example, do not threaten to take away a child's lunch if he cannot sit in his seat. You will not be able to follow through with it (because you must feed the child), and he will now know that you cannot be taken at your word.

- **Keep it simple.** When setting a routine, keep it simple and do what comes naturally. Making the routine too detailed or complicated will create more discipline problems than it will solve.

Setting a daily routine and establishing rituals means less confusion. If we do things the same every day, then no one is confused about when we are going to play outside and when we will be doing art.

Planning Ahead

What child can resist a singing puppet, an opportunity to play on a musical instrument, or finger painting in every color of the rainbow? Sometimes, the best form of discipline is a fabulous curriculum. When you are prepared with a lesson that is developmentally appropriate, interesting, and engaging and have backup plans for when things go awry (and they often do), you will eliminate a whole category of misbehavior. Here are some tips to help you plan for better behavior.

- **Make sure that your curriculum is developmentally appropriate.** This means that the subject as well as the content should be geared to the age of the children that you are teaching. Adjusting so that lessons are neither too simple nor over their heads means that you will not lose their interest. Children who are interested are less likely to act out if they know that they will lose the opportunity to participate in an activity that they are looking forward to doing.

- **Set up before class.** Take time to get your room prepared before you begin the day. Organize your materials so that you have everything you need at your fingertips.

- **Have something quiet on hand.** Having a preplanned quiet activity gives you an alternative to offer a child who just cannot sit still or participate as expected. You will not have to break your rhythm while you search for an activity. Engage the child in something quiet, such as books, puzzles, or coloring pages, that will give him time to calm down and regroup. Having an extra alternative on hand will also help you control those children whose interest levels may not be the same as those of the rest of the group. Being able to give them an immediate choice may help them make good choices rather than find activities on their own that are poor ones.

- **Have backup activities ready.** Often, your activity will not go exactly as planned. Perhaps the project proved to be more difficult than you had anticipated, or the children's interest did not hold for as long as you had hoped. Overplanning your day will give you options to turn to when your original plans get thrown for a loop. You will be able to transition right from one activity to the next without missing a beat.

- **Weave variety into your plan.** If your daily plan calls for reading time, on top of circle time, on top of quiet centers, you may find yourself with a boisterous bunch that is ready to explode at a moment's notice. Plan your day so that quiet activities alternate with active times.

Assessing Individual Needs

Every child who enters your classroom is someone with individual needs. Those needs may change gradually or instantaneously. One child may be particularly wiggly. Another may need a little time to himself after being disciplined. Others may have disabilities or special circumstances and may need an extra dose of understanding. Knowing the children well, including their backgrounds, needs, and abilities, will help you support each child as an individual as they make behavior choices throughout the day. Knowing the children well will also help you set appropriate expectations. Read the Assessment section of this book (pages 6–60) for activities, milestones, and checklists.

- **Be aware of children as they come to school.** On any given day, the children come to your class carrying with them much more than their backpacks. They come with all of the experiences that they have had since they last saw you. Knowing who may be hungry, not feeling well, or even emotionally unstable from home experiences will help you make compassionate considerations as you interact with the children throughout the day. When children are off balance, they often do not behave as they usually would.

- **Every human being is born with a temperament.** Some are easygoing. Others are determined and opinionated. Some are outgoing and others are introverted. Knowing that we are all different and allowing for those differences will make your discipline strategy more successful. If you know what kind of temperaments you are dealing with, you can tailor your approach to get the best response and help each child learn a better way of behavior.

- **Assess individual activities.** Assess each segment of your day and ask yourself what behavior you would expect and what behaviors you will tolerate in each segment. Noisy, boisterous behavior during noisy, boisterous activities is fine. It is not appropriate during reading time.

- **Allow for flexibility.** As you know, all it takes is one small thing to overthrow a perfectly planned day. Snowflakes, a sick tummy, a special visitor, or a parent who "pops in" for a minute all have the potential to throw off what you have planned. Being willing to compromise and preparing for the inevitable will let you capitalize on those moments of surprise rather than let them turn your classroom upside down.

Solutions Throughout the Day

Throughout the day, there are key times when behavior has the potential to spiral out of control. There are times when being able to manage your group makes things go much more smoothly than they would have with no planning or preparation.

Having a specific routine for your day will help children know what is coming next. They can focus on playtime rather than when lunch might be. Having a routine is soothing to children. Knowing that they will be doing the same thing in the same order every day is comforting and reassuring.

Saying "hello" in the morning and "good-bye" in the afternoon can be especially tricky transition times. Providing helpful tips to families dealing with separation anxiety and transitional meltdown will make the beginnings and endings of your day as peaceful as the rest of the day.

Introduce the rules and role-play or demonstrate what each rule means. Refer to the classroom rules frequently and use the same language each time you refer to a rule. Use the classroom rules (pages 108–110), mealtime rules (pages 114–115), playground rules (pages 117–118), bathroom rules (pages 121–122), and nap time rules (page 124) to get started. Use the rules cards to create posters, flash cards, coloring books or pages, memory cards, and other activities to help children become familiar with each one. Be sure to state the rules positively. This tells children what they can do, not just what they cannot.

Finally, planning for those little in-between times—transitions between one activity and the next—makes all of the difference in your day. Keep a list of successful transition activities, such as favorite songs, finger plays, poems, and games, handy. Use the activities on page 127 for successful transitions. Take them one minute at a time, and you will be amazed at how much those little moments add up to a great day.

Classroom Rules

We sit at circle time.

We raise our hands when we want to talk.

We take turns and share.

We follow the teacher.

Classroom Rules

We line up straight without crowding or pushing.

We use kind words.

We clean up after ourselves.

We use inside voices in the classroom.

We are all friends.

We use walking feet inside.

There are times to talk and times to listen.

We wait for our turn.

Hello and Good-Bye Transitions

The two most difficult transitions that you will make each day are transitions from home to school and back again. For most children, this is a happy and easy event. They look forward to fun and friends at school. They come right in and get on with the business of being a preschooler. They are equally happy to see their families at the end of the day, so sending them home takes little more than helping them be prepared with backpacks loaded and jackets at the ready.

For others, transitioning into school can be a difficult and emotional event. Surviving separation anxiety (a child's fear of being separated from a loved one) takes patience, understanding, and sometimes nerves of steel. Here are some ideas to help you, the children, and their families cope.

- **Plan ahead.** Have several "soothing activities" (see page 112) ready so that there is something that the child can get busy with the minute he arrives in class. Knowing the special quirks or interests of each child will be helpful. Encourage family members to prepare their child by talking positively and reassuringly about school.

- **Reassure family members that their child will be fine.** Separation anxiety rarely lasts more than a few minutes. Let them know that you have dealt with this many times. Encourage them to call the school if they have any concerns or want confirmation that their child has calmed down and is happily engaged.

- **Use photo boards.** Create and laminate a picture board showing steps for children to follow when they enter in the morning and throughout the day. A picture of a child hanging up her coat, putting away her backpack, etc., will help keep children focused as they transition from home to school and back home again.

- **Prepare family members to make quick good-byes.** Lingering with a clinging or crying child will not make the transition any easier. A hug, a kiss, and a quick good-bye will make the best of the situation. Read *The Kissing Hand* by Audrey Penn (Tanglewood Press, 2006), and talk about special family rituals, traditions, or other ways that the children can overcome their separation anxiety.

Transitional meltdowns happen when a child is dropped off or picked up from school and, seizing the moment, turns into an unruly child. Remember too that at this time the child is testing limits and trying to see who is in charge, the family member or the teacher. These moments can be doubly awkward because you and the family member may be wondering the same thing. Who is in charge of discipline during this transitional time when both family member and teacher are present? The easy and consistent answer to this is that as long as a child is at school, you are the front line for discipline. Be assertive and take the lead.

Soothing Activities

Having quiet activities ready will help a child transition into the classroom or soothe frayed nerves that arise during the day. Try these easy activities to help calm children during stressful times of the day.

- **Manipulatives:** Any small object that can be stacked, sorted, strung, or manipulated can be a soothing release. Twisting chenille stems into shapes, stringing beads, or stacking blocks are quiet activities that children can do by themselves or with a trusted friend.

- **Listening to stories:** Find a quiet, pillowed corner to sit and listen to storybooks on digital media.

- **Clay or play dough:** Having something soft and squishy to mold, roll, cut, and pound can work out frustrations.

- **Paper and crayons:** Drawing a picture for someone special or the simple, rhythmic strokes of coloring can soothe a child who has had trouble separating. Be sure to have children talk about the pictures that they drew.

- **Cleaning:** Many children find cleaning to be a calming activity. Set her aside with a bowl of warm, soapy water and let her scrub away her troubles.

- **Special detail:** Give a child who is having trouble fitting in a special job, such as handing out stickers or taking the mail to the office. He will feel important. We all feel better when our minds are occupied by doing things for someone.

- **Lap time:** Even big five-year-olds appreciate a little lap time. Sometimes, just being held close can be a calming experience. Snuggle as long as you can.

- **Cornmeal tracing:** Cover the bottom of a baking pan with cornmeal or flour and let the child spend time tracing or swirling the cornmeal with her fingers. Encourage her to write letters or shapes that she knows.

- **Drop by drop:** Give the child a jar of colored water, an empty jar, and an eye dropper. See how long it takes him to partially fill the second jar.

- **Share secrets.** Take the child aside and tell her that you have a secret you will share with her if she will share one with you. Whisper something about upcoming activities that she will be excited about, or simply say, "You are special to me." Then, give her a chance to share a secret with you.

- **Pet report:** Have the child spend some time observing a class pet. After a minute or two, have him give a pet report.

Mealtime

Placing a classroom of children in charge of food and liquid seems like a crazy idea that no one should attempt. Yet, this is exactly what you do each day at snack time or lunchtime. Setting children up for success means making sure that they have the skills and the preparation for taking care of themselves. Here are some suggestions to make your eating times go more smoothly.

- **Manners matter.** Teach children early to say "please," "thank you," and "no, thank you." Manners matter, especially when you are eating in a public setting. Encourage children to follow basic manners, like taking small bites, speaking only when their mouths are clear of food, and chewing with their mouths closed. Not only will you have a more pleasant meal, but you will avoid complications like choking because someone did not chew food well enough.

- **Use quiet voices.** Using quiet voices allows children the opportunity to converse without things being so noisy that you cannot give directions or warnings. As the talk begins to escalate, quiet children back down. Separate children who are having an especially difficult time keeping their voices in check.

- **Trying new foods:** Mealtime is an opportunity for an adventure. There may be many times when children are served foods that they do not like. Encourage children to try new things. Talk about the foods and the different food groups or health benefits of each one as they eat each day. Encourage children to eat their own food. Sharing food can sometimes lead to sharing unwanted things, like germs.

- **Stay seated.** Encourage children to stay seated and raise their hands if they need help. Children moving about increases the potential for spills and accidents.

- **Clean up.** Have the necessary tools available so that children can clean up on their own. Have an empty garbage can ready, along with a wiping cloth and cleaner for spills.

- **Special seating:** Have a special place for children who are having trouble eating and following the rules. If one child is disrupting fellow diners, move her to where she can eat quietly on her own.

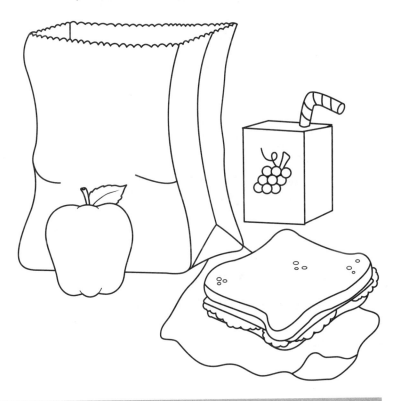

Mealtime Rules

We wash our hands before we eat.

We raise our hands if we need help.

We eat our own food and try everything on our plates.

We stay in our seats.

114

**We clean up
after ourselves.**

Food stays on our plates.

We use quiet talking voices.

**We wait for our friends to
finish eating.**

Playground Rules and Safety

One of the favorite times of day for most children is the opportunity for free play outside. Finally, they can run, jump, shout, stretch, try, and try again. Outdoor play provides a variety of essential skill-building opportunities, from the enjoyment of nature to gross motor development. Outdoor play is a treasure trove of learning. Yet, the playground can be one of the most dangerous spots for children to be. With proper supervision and attention to rules and safety, you can provide children with this important opportunity for growing.

- **Make sure that the equipment is safe and in good repair.** Check each piece regularly for missing or loose screws and other hazards. These might potentially cause injury, choking, or strangulation.

- **Use appropriate equipment.** Make sure that the equipment that children are using is age appropriate. If they are using swings or climbing equipment intended for older children, or tricycles that are too small, the potential for injury increases.

- **Rehearse the playground rules often.** When you see a rules infraction, stop the child immediately, recite the rules, and then make sure that the child follows these rules. Post the rules where children can refer to them often.

- **Be vigilant.** Wander through the playground throughout the play period. Keep your eyes on the children as they play. Make sure that you can see everyone, and never leave them alone, even for just one minute. If you can, be sure to have help if you have a large group.

- **Watch for unsafe play.** Allow children the opportunity to run and have fun, but make sure that it does not escalate to the point of potential danger to a child. Provide alternatives for children who cannot refrain from inappropriate behavior.

- **Give a wind-down warning.** Give a five-minute warning so that children who are waiting for turns on the swings or who are engaged in other play will have time to finish before it is time to go inside.

- **Use a timer or whistle to get children's attention.** Have a buzzer or whistle to indicate to children that it is time to stop and come in. Give rewards to those children who can line up by the time that you count to 10.

- **Make sure that children are appropriately dressed for weather and safety.**

Playground Rules

**We pay attention
to the weather.**

**We sit in the swings and
hold on tightly.**

**We climb up the ladder and
go down the slide.**

**We let our teacher know
if we need to go inside.**

We play where our teacher can see us.

We share. We take turns. We play fairly.

Balls are for throwing, rolling, and kicking safely to our friends.

Sand and toys stay on the ground.

Cleanup

It always seems like the more fun that children have, the more there is to clean up. Getting children to take responsibility for their own messes is an important skill to teach. Keeping them engaged and interested in cleanup may seem difficult, as the next activity may be more enticing than cleaning.

- **Give fair warning.** Your request for cleanup will meet with a substantial amount of resistance if you spring it on children when they are in the middle of playtime. Give them a five- and then a two-minute warning to let them wind down and finish up what must be finished before moving on.

- **Clean as you go.** Do not wait until the last minute to clean up. Encourage children to clean up as they go so that they will not have a big job at the end of the project.

- **Sing a song.** Encourage quick cleanups by singing a favorite song to see if the class can finish cleaning up by the time that you are done with the song.

- **Get organized.** Make sure that there is a place for everything to be put away. Provide bins or boxes for collections of small toys. Label shelves to match the boxes.

- **Reward cleaners.** Saying things like, "I can see Joey cleaning up" not only makes Joey proud and a more determined cleaner, but also makes the other children work hard just to hear their names called too.

- **Break it up into simple tasks.** If there are multiple layers of cleanup to be done, assign children different tasks so that each child has responsibility for one part.

- **Everyone works until it is done.** When a child finishes cleaning in his area, encourage him to help his friends in another area. Give an award for the best "cleaner-upper" of the day.

- **Spring clean on a regular basis.** Do not wait for things to become excessively dirty before you break down and clean. Let children help you soap up the toys, wash windows, fix books, and wipe tables, walls, and doors. Be sure to watch the cleaning supplies and make sure that they are safe for use around children.

 **(See page 2.)**

- **Do not do it for them.** If a job is not done satisfactorily, call them back to try it again.

Bathroom Rules, Manners, and Hygiene

Children need continued instruction in appropriate bathroom behaviors, particularly if this is their first experience in school. Going to the bathroom in a public place can be a daunting experience. But, knowing what to do means more independence and less mess left behind. The following are some ideas to help make sure that each child can navigate the bathroom experience successfully.

- **Model appropriate behavior.** Walk through each step of the process by familiarizing children with the bathroom rules (see pages 121–122) and acquainting them with the equipment in the bathroom.

- **Not for play:** Remind children that the bathroom is not a place for play. When they need to use the bathroom, or when the class is taking a potty break, their job is to get in and out as quickly as possible.

- **Ask for help.** Children need to know how to handle emergencies that may arise. They need reassurance that you are available to help with sticky snaps and buttons, and that you need to know immediately if a toilet or sink is clogged, will not flush, or is overflowing.

- **Wash hands.** One of the most important steps in the bathroom process is getting in the habit of washing hands with warm water and soap. Hang a hand washing chart showing step-by-step photos. If a child forgets, send him back.

- **Clean up.** Each child should be responsible for cleaning up after himself. Show children how to use just a little toilet tissue and make sure that it goes down the toilet when they flush. Demonstrate how to rinse out the sink if they have left dirt behind. Remind them that paper towels go in the trash can, not in the toilet or on the floor.

- **Group potty stops:** Occasionally, it will be necessary for you to have a time when all of the children take a potty break at the same time, such as before outside play or nap time. Encourage each child to try to use the bathroom, whether or not he feels that he needs to. Chances are that the urge will come in a few minutes, at a less convenient time. Keep the other children occupied with songs or finger plays while you are waiting for everyone to finish up.

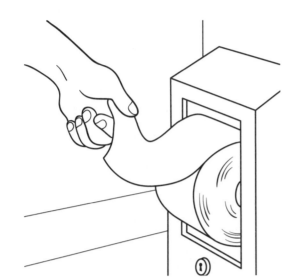

We use just enough toilet paper to get the job done.

We flush.

One person uses the sink or the potty at a time.

We wash our hands with soap and water.

Bathroom Rules

We clean up after ourselves.

We turn off the water.

**We get the job done
and then leave.
Bathrooms are not for playing.**

**We let our teacher
know when we are
finished using the bathroom.**

Nap Time

Nap time can be a challenging time of the day. Sometimes, just getting one child to lie down and rest can be an exhausting experience, not to mention having a whole room of wiggly bodies to quiet. Providing the right atmosphere and backup plans for those who cannot sleep will make nap time as smooth and successful as possible.

- **Slow down.** Do not rush into nap time. Take a few moments for some quiet time. Read a story, do some relaxation and stretching exercises, or give children one last opportunity for some share time before they lie down.

- **Last call:** Provide one last opportunity to get a drink of water and use the bathroom. Have children remove their shoes and place them by their mats.

- **Quiet the room.** Darken the room as much as possible. Play soft, relaxing music to set the mood. Make sure that the temperature is set at a moderate level, not too hot or too cool.

- **Use soft, quiet voices.** Use a soft whisper and encourage children to keep their bodies and mouths from making noises too.

- **Read a story.** Read or tell a quiet story while children lie on their mats and drift off to sleep.

- **Separate children who disrupt.** Make sure that children who do not sleep are not lying next to one another. If possible, make sure that there is enough space between nap mats so that children cannot reach each other.

- **Have quiet activities to do if some children cannot fall asleep.** Book reading, puzzles, file folder games, flannel board games, and coloring are soothing activities for a child to do on his mat.

More Suggestions

Give children who cannot sleep something to think about.

- What makes you happy?

- What is your favorite toy?

- What would happen if you could fly?

- If you could be an animal, what would you be?

- Where do you think you will go today after school?

- What is the nicest thing that someone has done for you?

Nap Time Rules

We lie quietly on our mats.

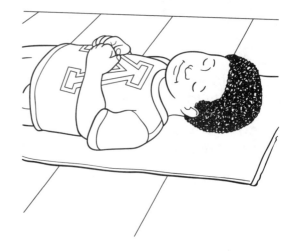

**We close our eyes
and try to rest.**

**We are quiet even
if we are not sleepy.**

**Others are trying to sleep.
If we must talk, we whisper.**

Wiggling

If you have spent more than a few minutes with a preschooler, you know that they are wigglers. The need to be in constant motion is a hallmark of any child old enough to move. What do you do with all of that energy? Turn it into fun!

Before you begin circle time or story time, you will have much more success if you give children a chance to wiggle all of the wiggles away. When you notice the group getting restless or starting to lose interest in a lesson, pull out a favorite wiggling activity to help them refocus. If you can catch them before they lose control, you can stretch their attention spans and keep them engaged for longer periods of time. Here are some fun wiggling activities.

Rubber Bands

Have children pretend that their arms and legs are rubber bands. They s-t-r-e-t-c-h them out and then let them snap right back in. Try this stretching activity using different limbs and body parts, including ears, neck, fingers, and back. Be sure to have them say, "Boing!" as their rubber band arms snap back into shape.

Wiggly Worms

Have children sing "I'm a Wiggly Worm" while wiggling around on the ground.

I'm a Wiggly Worm

(Sing to the tune of "I'm a Little Tea Pot")

I'm a wiggly worm
Watch me go.
First, I wiggle to,
Now, I'll wiggle fro.
When I get all wound up
In a knot,
I'll wiggle right back
And find my spot.

Wiggle Hat

Fill a hat with several activity cards. Pull an activity card from the hat and have children do the activity suggested on the card. Pull them out one at a time, or select two or three to be done together. For example, if you pull cards that say *wiggle*, *roll*, and *jump*, children would wiggle, roll, and jump in order until you give the signal to stop. Pull out the wiggle hat any time you need a suggestion for wiggling.

Wiggle Sport

Divide the group into two teams. Place one team on one side of the room and the other team on the opposite side. Using the common sports cheer, "We've got spirit, yes we do! We have spirit, how about you?", have the two teams compete in wiggle sport. Start by having one side chant and clap,

"We've got wiggles, yes we do! We have wiggles, how about you?"

The other team then repeats the chant to the first side.

The first team then chants:

"We've got more! Let's play wiggle sport!"

The second team sits in place and watches as the first team wiggles as hard and fast as they can for about 30 seconds. Have both teams return to their starting places and have the second group start wiggle sport this time.

Traveling Tickles

Have children sing "Traveling Tickle."

Traveling Tickle

I've got a tickle in my toe
So I'll wiggle it just so.
I'll wiggle and I'll waggle just until . . .
   (pause)
Oh! No!

I've got a tickle in my knee
And it's really bugging me.
I'll wiggle and I'll waggle just until . . .
   (pause)
Oh! No!

I've got a tickle in my thigh
And it makes me want to sigh.

I've got a tickle in my tummy
And it feels really funny.

I've got a tickle in my arm
And I think it's doing me some harm.

I've got a tickle in my neck
So I think I'd better check.

I've got a tickle in my head
And I'm beginning to dread.

I'll wiggle and I'll waggle just until . . .
I pass the tickle on to you!

Activity Transitions

Transitions are those times of the day when you move from one activity to the next. All it takes to master transitions is a little practice and creativity. Smooth transitions can change a group from an unruly mob to the most well-behaved group that will be the envy of every other teacher in the school. Here are some tips for mastering transitions and some fun transition ideas to get you started.

- **Lead, do not send.** When moving from one area to another, wait until everyone is ready and then lead your group to the new location. You will not be gathering children as they get distracted in transit, and you will be the first person in the room to set the standard for behavior at the new activity.

- **Send children off when they are calm.** When excusing children to line up or to go to another activity, be sure to wait for them to show you that they are ready.

- **One at a time:** Send children to the next activity one at a time. If you send a large group, you can expect a noisy and unruly herd.

- **Repeat choices.** If someone gets lost between point A and point B, repeat the directions so that she can get back on track again.

- **Keep them preoccupied.** When you give children something to do with their hands or something to focus on while they are moving, they will be less likely to get off track.

- **Give warnings ahead of time.** Before concluding any activity, give a warning to wind down and mentally and physically prepare for cleanup.

Transition Fun

- Have children pretend to put marshmallows on their feet, in their hands, and in their mouths as they walk.

- Have children line up with their arms on the shoulders of the child in front of them like a train.

- Have children sneak to the next activity on tiptoes.

- Have children walk backward, crawl, or crab walk from one location to the next.

- Have children march with stiff arms and legs like soldiers or robots.

- Have children take huge steps or baby steps as you moon walk, or see how slowly you can go.

Concentration Techniques

Encouraging young children to concentrate can be tricky! Their egocentric stages of development bring a delightful self-confidence, so that they love to talk about themselves, their accomplishments, and everything that spontaneously comes to mind.

Occasionally, children need complete quiet with no distractions. Cozy corners and quiet spaces are excellent tools for fostering this type of environment.

Music with simple and consistent melodies and tempos can promote concentration. Try playing background music during an activity and watch the children for comfort and concentration levels.

Encourage children to use good manners words if another child's actions are bothering them.

Some children find that conversation during tasks helps them focus. Other children need the opposite. Try to seat children near others with similar working styles.

Physical signs often reveal a heightened level of concentration. Some children will stick their tongues out a little while others silently fold their lips inward.

Nonverbal cues are often more powerful than verbal reminders for children to stay on task. At the beginning of an activity, explain that if you want to remind one of them to stay focused, you will gently put your hand on her shoulder.

Gathering

Gathering children is most successful when using different strategies for capturing and keeping their attention. Here are some ideas to try.

- Use carpet squares, mats, or a masking tape line to direct children.

- Place small tokens, treats, or pictures of what you will be talking about on the floor.

- Place name tags or pictures of children where you want each to gather.

- Sing songs such as "Here We Are Together," or have other rituals such as hand-clapping or a special whistle or bell.

Here We Are Together

(Sing to the tune of "Have You Ever Seen a Lassie")

Here we are together, together, together,

Here we are together in our preschool class.

(say the children's names as they come to the circle)

Here's _____ (child's name) and _____,

Now _____ and _____.

Come and play together in our preschool class.

(Repeat as needed to sing everyone's name as he joins the circle.)

Line Up Song

(Sing to the tune of "Frère Jacques—Are You Sleeping?")

Come and line up, come and line up,

_____ (child's name) and _____.

We're getting ready to go just now. I need to see you show me how.

1-2-3. Come to me!

(Repeat as needed to sing everyone's name as she joins the line at the door.)

Attention Grabbers

Want to regain control of the class? Be prepared with a variety of attention grabbers or class traditions like these.

"1-2-3! Eyes on me!"

"Repeat my clap." You clap a pattern, and then children clap the pattern.

ABCs of Common Behaviors

More often than not, you will meet the same behavior problems year after year, child after child. The following pages list common discipline problems that you are likely to encounter with preschool children. Each topic is addressed with specific ideas for improving behavior and helping children choose a better way.

Each discipline topic is broken into the following categories:

- **What's Going On Here?** This section looks at the psychology behind the behavior, or why children do what they do. You can treat the symptoms of some behaviors (what you see happening) and still have recurring problems because the root of the behavior (what really is happening) has not been resolved. Understanding how a behavior gets started and its progression is helpful in eliminating poor behavior choices.

- **Management Ideas That Work:** Each topic in this section has management tips and suggestions for disciplining and changing behaviors. Several ideas of what to do and occasionally what *not* to do are included.

- **Let's Talk About It:** This section includes phrases that you can use as part of your behavior management strategy.

- **Let's Play Together:** This section includes games, activities, or projects that you can do with a child to help him learn a better way of behaving.

- **Let's Work Together:** Working on solutions together as a class is an important piece of your discipline plan. This section suggests ways that you can engage the whole class in learning appropriate behavior choices.

Use the behavior management charts (pages 69–72) and classroom (pages 108–110), mealtime (pages 114–115), playground (pages 117–118), and bathroom rules (pages 121–122) as needed to help reinforce positive behaviors and learning.

Aggressive Play

What's Going On Here?

Children need opportunities to express fears, experiment with power, and release energy. Rough or aggressive play happens in large part because of this. Children often try to assert their power and assess how much power they have. Aggressive play is a sign that a child's need for some form of release or relief is not being met.

Management Ideas That Work

Stop and assess the situation. Do the children need some time outdoors or a wiggling activity to use up some energy? Is a particular child acting out of frustration? Are there particular children in the class who are prone to aggressive play behavior and need an extra eye during free play times?

Aggressive play rarely starts out that way. It tends to escalate, so aggressive play should never be ignored. Stop aggressive play immediately, redirect the children who are involved, and show them how they can play, use their imaginations, and still be in control. Offer other forms of energy release, such as running or other physical activity.

Let's Talk About It

"We can run and chase when we're outside."

"Tristan doesn't want to play with you like that. Play gently or choose another game to play."

Let's Play Together

Run, run, run. Blow off steam. Have children run from one end of the playground to the other, or see how many times they can circle the playground. See if they can hop 100 times, jump over a spinning rope, or duck under or over other obstacles.

Show what "gentle" means by modeling gentle behavior with stuffed animals or by touching the child gently on the arm or shoulder.

Let's Work Together

Children who are the victims of aggressive play need skills to cope with an aggressor. Teaching children "brave talk" will give them solutions to take care of themselves. Saying, "I don't like that. Stop it now," like he means it draws the line. If someone still will not stop, then he can retreat to you as a second line of defense.

Arguing

What's Going On Here?

Some children seem to have something to say about everything, and others are not willing to take any directive easily. Children who are argumentative are usually looking for attention. Children crave adult attention, and some are willing to take it any way they can get it, even negatively.

Occasionally, children argue in an effort to question your authority or assert their own power. They push against the limits just to see how far they can get before someone will stop them.

Management Ideas That Work

Do not argue with a child or group of children. If children are acting innappropriately, you are only rewarding them by giving them the attention that they are seeking. Ignore them if possible, or respond in a nonemotional tone that you will get back to them later.

If all else fails, give them just enough information to stop the conversation. State rules simply, stick to routines, and be firm. Making sure that they understand the rules and that they must always follow them takes you out of the conversation. Making statements, such as "Because I said so," feeds a child with adversarial ammunition to challenge you. If it is not a matter of following rules, being flexible enough to let a negotiator offer a reasonable solution allows him the opportunity to control what he can in a setting that you are comfortable with.

Let's Talk About It

"I don't feel like talking about this now."

"How can we make this situation good for you and for me?"

Let's Play Together

Role-playing is almost always productive. Have him give you a command, such as "Please get me a book." You should then begin to argue with him and use every excuse imaginable. Talk about how unproductive arguing is, and how he can ask politely when he wants something.

Let's Work Together

As a class, make a list of things that the class can make choices about and things that they do not have as a choice. Offer alternatives to exercising choices so that the children will be prepared when these are presented to them.

Bossiness

What's Going On Here?

Some children are bossy because they enjoy the attention and the feeling of power. They erroneously believe that people do what they say because they like them or that they really do know better than everyone else. Other times, children are bossy because they have a need to have everything go in an ordered way or because they lack self-esteem. The notion that the only way to get people to do what you want is to be bossy to them comes from missed social cues and feelings of inadequacy. Being bossy is a habit that can lead to isolation or even evolve into bullying if left unchecked.

Management Ideas That Work

Redirecting a bossy child takes time and consistency. A bossy child needs to be shown how to approach other children appropriately when she has wants or needs. For example, if she wants someone to play with, she needs to be coached about how to ask a friend to play.

Help her choose a friend to play with and then model conversation so that they both can negotiate how and where to play together. As she gains confidence in herself, you will have to intervene less.

If a child is being bossy to you or other children, help her rephrase her commands appropriately as questions so that "Tie my shoes!" becomes "I need help with my shoes. Could you help me, please?"

Let's Talk About It

"Try again. Ask me nicely and I'll consider it."

"It's my job to be the teacher, and it's your job to learn. I'll let you know when I need your help."

Let's Play Together

Who is in charge? Get several pictures of organizations or businesses in your area. Include pictures of a home, police and fire stations, a classroom, and a store. Have the child tell you who is in charge in each place. Imagine what might happen if someone else took over the grocery store. Explain that we all have jobs—teachers teach, firefighters put out fires, and children play. Have her draw a picture of herself.

Let's Work Together

Play games like "Follow the Leader" or give children jobs for the day so that each child has an opportunity to be in charge.

Contagious Behavior

What's Going On Here?

Children love to mimic others' behaviors. If they see something that looks like it might be fun, children often have few inhibitions about joining in and trying it for themselves. Often, the instigator in contagious behavior is a child who has lost interest or has been temporarily distracted. The rest of the class may have trouble distinguishing whether the activity is part of a circle time activity, so they join in for the fun of it.

Management Ideas That Work

Once the ripple effect has started, it is hard to stop. The most effective way to recapture children's attention is to have a hand signal, special finger play, or some other signal that lets them know that they need to refocus their attention on you. Once you have regained their attention, you can restate rules and rejoin your lesson plan.

Let's Talk About It

"1-2-3, eyes on me!"

"Let's see who can be the first to be back in her place and listening."

Let's Play Together

Try this following directions game. Have the child sit across from you. Give him a direction for an activity and tell him that he is to do only that activity until you tell him to stop with a predetermined signal. Warn him that you will be trying to distract him to see how long he can follow your directions. For example, tell him to sit quietly and not smile. You will then do everything you can to get him to smile. Give a sticker or other reward if he stays true to your first direction.

Let's Work Together

Be the stopper. Tell children that you are going to give one of them a special button. This button is the stopper. No one but the person who has the stopper should know who has it, so remind them not to show it to anyone. Have the children sit in a circle and pretend to pass the button to everyone, but exchange it with only one. Tell the class that you are going to whisper a direction in someone's ear. They will then do the activity (such as stomp feet). Then, everyone else in the circle will follow them. Everyone, that is, except the child with the stopper. The object is to try to guess who the stopper is by watching for the child who is still sitting quietly. Talk about helping each other follow the rules by looking for the one who is following the rules rather than those who are not.

Defiance

What's Going On Here?

There are many reasons why children are defiant. Changes going on at home, such as a new baby, divorce, and remarriage, or feeling tired, frustrated, hungry, bored, or neglected can lead to defiance. These are all reasons why children become defensive and begin to challenge authority. The preschool years are key for learning about personal power. Children spend a good deal of their time trying to establish what they can and cannot do through trying and learning new skills. They also try questioning authority to see what the limits are.

Management Ideas That Work

Stay calm. Catch a defiant child off guard by reacting in the opposite way from what she is expecting.

Determine what is at the root of the defiance. Once you know what is driving the defiance, you can address it and work together to find an amicable resolution. Be firm, let her know what you expect, offer choices, and then give a time limit for compliance. If she still will not cooperate, then some time alone to think about it or a loss of privilege is appropriate. If a child shows signs of defiant behaviors over a long period of time and does not respond to behavior management techniques, professional evaluation may be in order.

Let's Talk About It

"This is not a choice."

"You can choose, or I will choose for you."

Let's Play Together

Try this following directions practice. Play a game asking the defiant child to identify different times that it is fine to say no, and times when it is not fine to tell a teacher (or family member) no. Next, tell her that you are going to give her a direction. If she follows it the first time, you have a surprise for her. Give a direction, such as walk backward to the door and back. After she complies, give a big hug or some other token to reward good behavior.

Let's Work Together

Read *Cows in the Kitchen* by June Crebbin (Candlewick, 2003), and talk about the barnyard animals' decision not to follow the farmer's directions. What might have been averted had they listened to the farmer?

Destructive Play

What's Going On Here?

Obviously, accidents happen. Children have a natural interest in cause and effect. Other times, property gets destroyed when it is used improperly. Some children have an impulsive nature and break things before their brains have time to react and tell them to stop. But, a deliberate act that destroys property is a behavior issue that should be addressed immediately.

Management Ideas That Work

Predict it, see it, stop it, and redirect. Explain what will happen if destructive play continues. Most children are willing to stop without complaint.

If a child does break or destroy classroom equipment, have her clean it up or repair it if it is safe and possible. Encourage her to apologize to her classmates. Give her an opportunity to "work it off" to pay for the broken game by cleaning or fixing another part of the classroom.

Let's Talk About It

"We want to keep our toys nice."

"If we can't play nicely, then we'll have to put it away."

Let's Play Together

Make a game of looking for items around the room that need attention (cleaning, repairing, or replacing missing pieces). Talk about how, if things are broken, playing with them is impossible.

Let's Work Together

Plan a lesson to present supplies, manipulatives, and equipment as treasures that you all share. Have children give you ideas of what they can do to take care of their treasures. Show children how to take care of each item in the classroom. Give each one the responsibility of a piece of equipment or item to watch over and monitor.

Friends (Cooperating, Sharing, and Respecting Others)

What's Going On Here?

As children develop from toddlers into the preschool years, they begin to take an interest in other children. They want to play with other children, but may not yet have the skills to know how to engage in a group activity or how to share items. Young children are very egocentric, which means that they see themselves as the center of the world. Learning to share and think about the needs of others are the first steps out of this little bubble that all children create around themselves.

Management Ideas That Work

Model or role-play different scenarios such as sharing, cooperating, taking turns, initiating play or addressing differences of opinion. Talk about how good it feels to have friends and how we can work together to have fun. As you see children playing peacefully, praise them. Let them know specifically how their play is friendly.

If you have continued squabbles, consider whether there are too many children in one area. If there is one instigator who needs time playing on her own, help her design better play strategies. Let each child express what the problem is. Restate the issues for the children so that they can consider the other's needs and design a solution to working together.

Let's Talk About It

"How can we work together to solve this?"

"What can you do about that?"

"I really like how well you are playing together!"

Let's Play Together

Play a sharing game together. Give every child a small bag of stickers or other small treat. Divide the class into small groups of two or three. Have children count the items in their bags and then divide them by sharing "one for you and one for me." Or, have them combine all of their bags and then pass out the items equally. Remind children that it is always more fun to share with friends.

Let's Work Together

Gather a selection of favorite storybooks about sharing and friends, such as *The Boy Who Wouldn't Share*, by Mike Reiss (HarperCollins, 2008). Talk about how the characters in the story learned to cooperate, share, and work together as friends.

Helplessness

What's Going On Here?

There are many reasons why a child might act helpless. He may get babied or may not have had a lot of opportunities to do for himself at home. He may not know that he can be independent yet. He may be suffering from a poor self-concept. He may truly believe (or have been carelessly told) that he cannot do for himself. Finally, and most commonly, he may be looking for a little extra attention.

Management Ideas That Work

Let him take care of himself. Try never to do something for a child that he can do for himself. You are just reinforcing the act of helplessness or the efforts to manipulate you into enabling this behavior. Break the task into small steps. Encourage the child to try each step until the task is completed. Give him attention when he is trying, not when he is complaining that he cannot. Give rewards and incentives to reach the solution on his own.

Have the proverbially helpless child help another child complete a task. He may be willing to do for someone else what he says he cannot do for himself.

Let's Talk About It

"You're getting so big! I know you can do it!"

"You start. Show me how much you can do. I'll help if you get stuck."

"I know you can do this."

Let's Play Together

Make an "I am getting so big!" booklet for each child. As children complete milestones, such as putting on their coats or shoes by themselves, add these skills to their books.

Let's Work Together

Use positive peer pressure to help encourage children to try new things. Have one child tell about something that he can do. Have all of the other children see if they can do it too. Give high-fives or hugs all around for the things that everyone can do.

Hurting or Other Out-of-Control Behaviors

What's Going On Here?

Children lash out for a number of reasons. Usually it is because they feel stretched beyond their limits. They are tired, frustrated, or hungry and do not have the verbal tools to deal with the anger, so they lash out.

Management Ideas That Work

Your first priority in dealing with a child who is screaming or hurting others is the safety of all of the children. Keep calm and remove or restrain the child if necessary.

Children are often scared about being out of control and scared about receiving discipline. In order to help them regain composure, offer choices. For example, a child who is screaming to get your attention will get it if she chooses to stop screaming. She is totally in control of whether or not you respond to her. Letting her see this connection will stop the behavior more quickly. A child who does not like being restrained can regain control when he can show you that he has control.

Help children learn the difference between accidents and "on purpose." If someone accidentally bumps another, a simple apology is all that is needed. Retaliation or willful hurting requires immediate removal. If another child has been hurt, give that child the necessary attention. Hurting others says that a child needs some time on her own to calm down and think about playing appropriately with others. Have a safe place or some quiet, soothing activities to help a child unwind. You may need to offer some way to work off all that frustration, such as scribbling on paper.

Let's Talk About It

"We are all friends. Use your words, not your fists."

"Screaming hurts my ears. I will sit with you when you can stop screaming."

Let's Play Together

Sometimes, in the process of unwinding, a child needs an opportunity to talk, but not with anyone who will respond. Give him a puppet or a stuffed animal to confess his frustrations to. When he is finished talking, he can tell you what he and his stuffed buddy decided.

Let's Work Together

Talk about what is OK and what is not OK in avoiding hurtful behavior.

Ignoring and Not Following Directions

What's Going On Here?

One of the most frustrating things for a teacher is to give directions and have no one follow them. The children may be bored with what they are learning or distracted by other interesting subjects. There may be so many distractions that they really cannot hear you. Sometimes, children ignore teachers on an individual level as a passive-aggressive way to say no. Other times, they may feel that if they ignore you, they can pursue their own interests.

Management Ideas That Work

Make sure that the children can see you. Look to see that they are listening, or have some signal, such as a bell or a raised hand, to show that they are all paying attention. (See page 129 for attention-grabbing activities.)

Vary your voice. Instead of getting louder, whisper. Sing your instructions. Stop talking altogether and use hand signals.

Have a child repeat the directions back to you so that you know that he got it.

Get down on the child's level.

Give just one direction at a time. Repeat directions as necessary.

Offer rewards or praise when children are listening. If others feel that they are missing out on something, they will join in.

Let's Talk About It

"I need to see your face so that I know you're listening."

"You need to listen so that you don't miss something important."

"Focus your eyes, zip your lips, and turn on your listening ears."

Let's Play Together

Tell a child that you are going to give her three directions, such as sit, clap your hands, and jump in the air. She will have to listen carefully and then remember. Give her a reward for each direction that she completes and increase the number of directions as she succeeds.

Let's Work Together

Can you hear me? Tell the children that you are going to say something. If they hear you, they should raise their hands and tell you what they heard. Give simple statements in a quieter and quieter voice until you are barely using a whisper.

Lying

What's Going On Here?

Children lie for a number of reasons. One reason is for convenience—it is easier to lie than to try to explain yourself. Another reason children lie is to avoid being punished. A third reason is because the boundaries of what is real and what is not are still being formed during the preschool years. Two children can be in the same situation and have very different views about what happened.

Management Ideas That Work

Let the child know that you realize that he is not telling the truth. Allow him to explain himself. Talk about what being honest is and what a lie is. Have him apologize to the other parties if others are involved. Stress that you always expect the truth. Hold the child accountable. Even if he is afraid of getting in trouble, he needs to know that lying is unacceptable.

When two children have differing opinions, let them both share their sides of the story so that you can assess where truth and fairness lie. Ask them to tell you what happened, rather than confronting them with a "Did you _____?" question. They will be able to express themselves more clearly and will not be backed into a corner that they cannot get out of. Do not call in witnesses to verify a testimony. You will be setting up a pattern of distrust between you and the child or children.

Let's Talk About It

"Tell me what happened."

"I don't think you're telling me the truth. Would you like to try again?"

Let's Play Together

Sit with a child and take turns telling stories. Have the listener guess whether what is said is the truth or a lie. Give him a hug when he tells you a truth.

Let's Work Together

Read *The Berenstain Bears and the Truth* by Stan and Jan Berenstain (Random House Books for Young Readers, 1983) and talk about what might happen when we do not tell the truth.

Nonparticipation

What's Going On Here?

A sidelined child could be the result of fatigue, shyness, a bad mood, or an offense from a classmate. Often, nonparticipation signals a child who needs attention.

Management Ideas That Work

Typically, this child acts as though he would rather be alone. But, deep down he knows that you care enough to give him the attention that he needs and that you will try to engage him in the activity. If this is the case, acknowledge his choice not to participate, encourage him to rejoin you, and then move on. The more attention you pay to this type of behavior, the more you will see it not only with this child but also with others.

If the child is shy, he will slowly become acclimated and join in the fun when he is ready. Encourage him to try a part of the activity without having to jump in headfirst. If the child is in a bad mood, allowing him a few minutes to himself to sort things out is the best thing that you can do for him.

If you find that several children are opting out of activities, you may want to reevaluate your curriculum. They may have outgrown your lessons or may be ready for new challenges.

Let's Talk About It

"I'd like you to try it. I think you'll like it."

"Maybe you'll join us later."

Let's Play Together

Encourage the child to participate with the class, and give him an opportunity to plan a future activity. You will get a sense of his comfort level, and it will be hard for him to resist an activity that he planned.

Let's Work Together

Encourage the other children to include the nonparticipant. Choose a friend to help transition him back into the activity.

Sassing

What's Going On Here?

Usually, sassing is the careless use of words that have been allowed without correction. Often, children mimic the sarcastic tones that they hear adults or older siblings use. Occasionally, sassing and sarcasm come from a child who feels hurt or defensive. But, know that sassing is a habit that can be broken when you hold children responsible for their words and respond only when they can address others appropriately.

Management Ideas That Work

Respond to sassing immediately. Let the child know that his words and tone are unacceptable. Help the child rephrase his words in a more appropriate manner. If sassing continues, a loss of privilege or a time-out is appropriate.

Watch your tone when addressing children. If you want the children to use appropriate words and tones, then you need to model that for them. In the same manner, do not allow children to speak disrespectfully or sass other children. Remind children to use only helping words in the class.

Let's Talk About It

"We use helping words in our class."

"I won't respond to that tone. When you can talk to me respectfully, I'll listen."

Let's Play Together

When a child has a problem with sassing, have her teach a doll or a teddy bear how to ask for things nicely or respond to disappointment without using sassy words. When she thinks that she has taught the doll correctly, have her help the doll demonstrate her new skills.

Let's Work Together

Play a variation of Mother, May I? Have one child stand on one side of the room. The other children should line up on the opposite side. Each child asks the person who is "it" a question, such as "May I take four steps forward?" The person who is "it" responds with "yes, you may" if the person remembers to ask nicely and uses "please." If children fail to say "thank you" after moving, they must return to the spot that they started from.

Talking Out of Turn

What's Going On Here?

Sometimes, interrupting behaviors happen in preschool because of the nature of children. They are exposed to many new and different experiences and ideas. So much of life is exciting, and you might mention something that sparks a memory or is meaningful, and they just cannot wait to share.

Management Ideas That Work

Try not to acknowledge the interruption by letting it stop what you are doing. Ignore it and move on. If the child is persistent, remind him that you are in the middle of something. Assure him that he will have an opportunity to share and to save his thought. Continue without stopping, but do remember to give children a chance to share when you are finished.

Before starting a lesson that will require longer periods of listening, give the children an opportunity to share ideas and talk.

Let's Talk About It

"Can you tell me this later?"

"It's my turn to talk now. You'll get your turn to share in a minute."

"Raise your hand if you want to share something."

Let's Play Together

Play the interrupting game. Sit across from the child knee to knee. Tell her that you are going to play an interrupting game. You are going to talk, and you want her to try to interrupt you. After playing, stop and ask what she heard you say. Chances are she will not be able to remember. Point out that when you interrupt, you are not getting the information that you need. Reverse it and have her talk while you interrupt. Talk about how frustrating it is to have someone talk while you are talking.

Let's Work Together

When sharing thoughts and ideas, call on children who are sitting quietly and have their hands raised. Roll a ball to the child that you have chosen. Remind the other children that if they do not have the "talking ball," it is their turn to listen.

Tattling

What's Going On Here?

If a child tattles to you that someone hurt her, took her toy, or offended her in some way, she is trying to get you to defend her. If a child is filling you in on every detail of others' behavior, he is trying to be informational. He may feel that he is being helpful.

If a child is tattling on misbehaviors in the classroom, she may be worried or afraid of something going wrong. She needs to know that you are aware and in control.

Management Ideas That Work

When a child tattles to you on her own behalf, ask her how she is going to handle it. Then, let her take care of it. She will be learning important life skills and will need to tattle less to you.

If a child is tattling on other children, reassure him that you are aware and that you want to hear only good information. "Tell me something good that's happening" often catches a child off guard.

If you have been inundated with tattling, offer a special time and place where tattles will be heard at a later time. Chances are they will be forgotten. When all else fails, turn the tables on the child. Tell her that your ears are full of tattles and hurt, and you do not have room for any more.

Let's Talk About It

"I'm so glad that you know what to do. You make good choices, don't you?"

"Tell me something good."

Let's Play Together

Have your prolific tattler see how many good things she can see other children doing.

Let's Work Together

What is telling, what is tattling? While tattles are annoying and rude, it is important for the class to know the difference between what is telling and what is tattling. Telling you when someone is hurt is OK. Telling you about someone else in order to get him or her in trouble is tattling. Make a list of different telling and tattling scenarios. Have children put their hands over their ears if it is tattling and raise their hands if it is telling.

Temper Tantrums

What's Going On Here?

Temper tantrums are a common behavior problem in the preschool years. When a child does not like what is going on and cannot do anything to change it, she is likely to have a meltdown. When a child has a temper tantrum, she is expressing anger and frustration over a situation she feels she has no control over. You have told her no, and she does not like it. Temper tantrums are more common with young preschoolers, as they are just learning how to express themselves verbally. A preschooler is more likely to throw a tantrum when she is tired, stressed, or hungry. As children grow and learn to negotiate or to put off impulses, temper tantrums subside.

Management Ideas That Work

Help children who have a tendency to have tantrums avoid putting themselves in situations where they will be vulnerable. If you know that asking her to clean up will set her off, give ample warning. Recognizing when a child is reaching his frustration level and then helping him regroup and calm down takes sensitivity and careful consideration of the individual needs of the children in your class.

If a child is having a full-blown tantrum, and if he is in no danger of hurting himself or others, simply walk away. Give children an opportunity to have control through making choices, not through manipulating or getting into a power struggle with you.

Let's Talk About It

"We'll talk about this when you are calm."

"You look like you are getting frustrated. What can I do to help?"

Let's Play Together

Gather several pictures of people who are happy, sad, or angry. Talk about the emotion in each picture and what the individual who is sad, frustrated, or angry can do to change what is making him feel that way.

Let's Work Together

You obviously will not be able to ignore tantrums easily, but stay as disengaged as possible. It is the key to success. If possible, remove the child and place him in a quiet spot in the room. If the child continues to disrupt, withdraw privileges and increase the amount of time in time-out.

"Ugly" Words

What's Going On Here?

Using inappropriate or potty words often begins innocently. Children have a natural curiosity about their bodies and the bathroom in general. They use these words with no real understanding of what they are saying. But, the shock on a family member's face or the giggles from playmates are enough to show that potty words get attention. Even negative attention is good attention some of the time. Of course, name calling is a more deliberate attempt to hurt another child's feelings. Children may be hurt, angry, or defensive and lash out using hurtful words.

Management Ideas That Work

Regardless of how shocking or humorous what you just heard may be, the less attention you can give a child when he is using questionable words, the more effective your discipline measures are going to be. A simple warning and a reminder of the consequences if ugly words are repeated, such as time-out, usually take care of the problem.

When a child reports to you that another child has called him names, help him work through it with his words. Follow up with something like, "Apparently _____ (the name-caller) does not know what he's talking about. Go use your brave talk and tell him to stop calling you names."

Let's Talk About It

"That's a word we don't use in the classroom."

"Those are hurting words."

Let's Play Together

Remind children that using ugly words and negative talk hurts someone's feelings. Have each person find something nice to say about the others in class.

Let's Work Together

Obtain a small garbage can with a lid. Draw a big frowning face on the side of the garbage can. Have a circle time lesson about helpful and hurting words. Write all of the words on slips of paper. Have children help you separate the good words from the bad words and feed the bad words to the garbage head.

Voice Volume

What's Going On Here?

Some children have voices that are naturally loud and will carry over a group of other voices without effort. But, when you are in a classroom full of children, it is important that children learn to control their voices so that others can play and converse. Some children may be sensitive to noise and feel that they have to talk over all of the other sounds that are competing for their attention. Typically, a child who talks loudly does so because he feels that he is not being heard. He may need help in negotiating and cooperating while playing with friends.

Management Ideas That Work

The first thing to do is to rule out hearing loss. A child may be compensating because he cannot hear how loud he is.

Give lots of gentle reminders. An effective way of doing this is by walking over to the child and whispering a reminder to use an inside voice.

Teaching children to take turns when talking helps them learn that louder does not always get their point across when someone else is talking too.

Let's Talk About It

"Please use your indoor voice."

"Quiet your voice. Your talking is so loud that it hurts my ears."

Let's Play Together

Try this activity called "Loud and Quiet Spots." Cut several large circles from red and green construction paper. Tape them on the floor around the room. Tell the children that all of the green circles are loud spots. When they stand on one of those, they can be as loud as they want or need to be. When they stand on one of the red circles, this is a quiet spot. When standing on a quiet spot, they need to use an inside, or quiet, speaking voice. At your signal, a child runs to a spot and sings the ABC song—softly if he is standing on red, loudly if he is on green. Repeat, removing spots as you go until there is only one red spot left in the room. Remind children that we use quiet voices inside. Let the child who is having trouble with volume carry a green spot and place it outside where it is OK to be loud.

Let's Work Together

At circle time, make a list of things that are loud and things that are quiet. Go outside and sing a favorite song in outside voices. Return to the classroom and repeat the song, this time with inside voices. Talk about the difference between a loud voice and a soft voice and when it is appropriate to use each.

Wandering

What's Going On Here?

Usually, if a child is wandering, it is because he does not yet know that it is not appropriate. This may be his first experience in preschool, and he may not be used to being restricted to one place. He may not be used to doing what others are doing instead of whatever he wants to do. Wandering can also be the result of a child losing interest. He may need a change of pace to keep him engaged in the group activity.

Management Ideas That Work

Quickly call the child back and remind him that he needs to stay seated. Stop and take occasional breaks for wiggling. Then, proceed with your lesson. You may have to physically redirect him to where he needs to be.

Seat wanderers close to you so that you can put a gentle hand on a shoulder if you sense movement. Use other management techniques, such as calling a child's name, or having a child take part in the lesson by holding a picture or leading the class in a song.

Let's Talk About It

"Stay on your bottom, please."

"This is our classroom. I'll let you know when it's time to leave."

Let's Play Together

Practice following rules by following directions. Give the child a command or direction and have him see how quickly he can follow. Reward with a sticker or hand stamp for following directions.

Let's Work Together

Encourage children to sit and stay focused by giving them clear directions of where you want them to be. Using carpet squares or other markers to let them know where to sit, and verbal reminders of the behavior you expect, will help children stay on task and in the right direction.

Whining and Complaining

What's Going On Here?

Typically, whining and complaining are attempts to gain attention that quickly turn into habits. Somewhere along the way, a whiner has learned that whining gets results. Deep down, a complainer whines because he does not feel understood. Whining is the means to getting what he wants rather than getting to the root of the problem.

Management Ideas That Work

The best line of defense against whining is a deaf ear. The less you can engage with a whiner, the less effective it will be. Ask her if she would like to repeat herself politely. If she persists in whining, make a blanket statement to let her know that when she whines, the answer will automatically be no. When the child is ready to talk without whining, listen carefully and rephrase her words to make sure that you understand what the real need is. Help her understand appropriate ways to express herself.

Asking a child what he intends to do about his complaint turns the responsibility back to the child to solve his problems and disengages you from the conversation. For innocuous complaints, have a special place, such as a corner or the bathroom mirror, where all complaints are to be registered.

Let's Talk About It

"We'll talk about this later when you can ask me nicely."

"You sound like you have a problem. What are you going to do about that?"

Let's Play Together

Play "Silent Whine." Have the child think about what he thinks he needs to whine or complain about. Tell him that the object of the game is to see if you can guess the complaint. The trick is to use only facial gestures, no words. If you cannot guess in five tries, have him tell you without whining. Then, trade places.

Let's Work Together

Play "Complaints at the Zoo." In addition to pretending to be zoo animals, see if the children can imagine them complaining. What would a lion or a mouse complain about? What would their voices sound like?

The Challenge Years

Every few years, it seems we are challenged with a group of children who provide more classroom management "opportunities" than we can imagine. Be encouraged! The design of this book is based upon consistency. Following a predictable rhythm of activities helps children know what to expect, and building confidence often builds positive behavior.

During the challenge years, it is wise to prepare the environment before the children even enter the room. Look, listen, and feel from the perspective that the children might as they walk in. Is the room adequately lit? Is the sunshine streaming in so brightly that it is blinding and causing irritating squinting? Is the air too hot or cold? Is the computer making a constant humming sound? Has the garbage been left, causing an annoying smell?

Before children enter, consider fostering a pleasant atmosphere for their senses. Plug in air fresheners. Play soft, peaceful instrumental music. Have small blankets or teddy bears available for extra hugs and snuggles.

As children enter the room, greet them with a verbal hello, a handshake, a high five, or a hug. Welcome them by name with a compliment or comment. Invest in a brief connection before the day begins.

Preparation is key in managing a group of young children. Boredom can beget misbehavior because children will challenge any "down" time with their own initiated activity. Display a picture in the room for children to focus on as they enter the room. This picture tells them what their first activity will be. After children complete the tasks of organizing for the day (hanging coats, backpacks, etc.), they know that there is a next-step activity expected. Often, using a silent sand timer helps motivate them to stay on task during activities throughout the day.

Getting children engaged immediately provides the freedom of having an extra few minutes to spend with the child who enters needing extra attention. Listening and helping diffuse some of the negative energy will offer a daylong payoff.

Children need to see your enthusiasm! Wear your favorite red shoes to school; post a positive mantra to constantly remind yourself of your "can do" attitude. Children will sense your tirelessness or tenseness, so do everything in your power to prove yourself capable and strong.

Give extra emphasis to basic classroom life skills like organization, taking turns, using classroom materials appropriately, and practicing self-regulation. You are not losing time by reviewing behavior skills. It is worth the investment. Learning cannot take place effectively if it is constantly being interrupted with behavioral concerns.

Instruction of basic life skills can include the five following themes: build-ups, active listening, truth, trust, and personal best. Reviewing them daily by reciting the following chant is a terrific reminder for children:

Build-ups, build-ups: Yes way!

Active listening: Hooray!

Truth and trust and personal best;

That takes care of all of the rest.

Have children snap their fingers while saying the chant. Often, little hands do not have the fine motor strength to snap, but pretending provides wonderful practice while building fine motor muscles. Most children love to pretend to snap, but if a child seems frustrated, encourage an alternative like patting her lap. The rhythm of the chant coupled with the snapping or patting fosters important prereading skills.

- **Build-Ups:** "Build-ups," the first idea in the above chant, is the positive turn on the directive, "No put-downs." Most children understand what a put-down is. Spend time discussing put-downs and model how children can change negative words into positive "build-ups." For example, a put-down would be, "Nikki, you never share the blocks. Give me some!" Ask the children how that would make Nikki feel. An alternative build-up comment might be, "Nikki, I like your tower. You are a good builder. Can I please have four blocks?" Little children need specific examples of situations that actually occur. Use their names and realistic conflicts to make practice more meaningful. Notice in the build-up example that compliments to Nikki and her project were given first. Next, four blocks were requested. Nikki will not feel threatened because she feels respected. She knows that her activity will not be taken over completely when only four blocks are needed.

- **Active Listening:** The second concept introduced in the chant is active listening. Review active listening ideas every time you transition into a new activity. Children love to brainstorm and share how active listeners use ears to listen or sit still with hands in laps. Many teachers ask children to sit with their legs crossed (like a pretzel) while being a good listener. Little ones love to add their own age-appropriate ideas.

- **Truth:** The third idea in the life skill chant is truth. Three- to five-year-old children are egocentric in thinking. Little "white lies" often seem perfectly fine to them. For example, when a teacher reminds a group to please stop talking, often a response of many little voices will chime, "I wasn't talking!" They so badly want to do the right thing and please adults that they are not able to objectively assess their own actions. Model and role-play opportunities to tell the truth from their point of view.

- **Trust:** Trust is the fourth idea in the chant. Due to their developmental stage, this may be a challenging concept to communicate. Examples for helping children understand trust might include: "I trust you to work together in picking up the connecting cubes"; "I trust that you will throw away your napkin after you finish your snack"; or "I like how you have shown me how I can trust you to let Jon tell his story without interrupting him." Rather than explaining the abstract ideas involved in trust, focus on describing specific actions.

- **Personal Bests:** The chant concludes with the idea of demonstrating personal best. Each child is a unique gift. Individual strengths and differences must be nurtured respectfully. What is one child's personal best will be quite different from another's. Helping children resist the temptation to compare is a lifelong lesson in developing self-satisfaction. To illustrate this idea to children, you may want to show a completed art project where two children show completely different outcomes. Praise each project using specific comments about how each shows that personal best was given. This is a wonderful tie-in to the first idea in the chant, build-ups.

After you have established a basic premise for appropriate classroom behavior, through the above chant or through your own method, continue successful classroom management with the following activities: standing up, singing loudly, singing instead of telling directions, and marching around the room to songs and chants suggested. Be creative! Children enjoy seeing a happy and silly teacher. Allowing silliness actually works as a terrific stress reliever. For example, when the volume in the room has reached an ear-piercing tone, shift class focus to a quick echoing activity where you alternate loud and soft sounds. Complete the echoing with a brief discussion of the necessity to lower the classroom volume.

Another stress-reliever for children is movement. In areas where weather dictates mostly indoor activity, children especially need gross motor release. Couple silly sounds with follow-the-leader trains or jumping jacks. Use the tables as tunnels to crawl through. Go on a tour of your building just to walk, skip, or jog.

On the opposite end of the spectrum, turning out the lights can offer a super stress-relieving moment as well. As the room is darkened, guide children in stretching their muscles. Teach them how to do push-ups and sit-ups properly. Deep muscle work, as done through squats or push-ups, uses a lot of energy, and it is often easier for children to refocus after.

While the lights are dimmed, teach other self-calming skills like controlled deep breathing through the nose and mouth. Ask them to breath in through their noses, hold it for several seconds, then slowly let the air back out through their mouths. They may giggle at first, but they become completely engaged as it takes concentration and effort. While relaxing, encourage children to give themselves "build-ups" inside their minds. For example, they can think to themselves, "I am a great kid!" and repeat the thought five times. As they count to five with their fingers, an important pre-math skill is being cultivated while regaining composure and classroom control.

Offer designated quiet areas in the classroom. When children feel the need to refocus, they can stretch out against large pillows, look through books, or color in journals. Listening centers are wonderful too. They are effective temporary escapes that also provide learning opportunities.

Music and song provide another avenue to regaining classroom control. Children instinctively respond to music when they might otherwise ignore spoken words. Test this theory by breaking into song when giving directions. The song "If You're Happy and You Know It" gives a versatile tune to almost any set of directions. One example is "If you're a good listener and you know it, eyes on me" (children whisper, "Eyes up").

Finally, try to keep yourself motivated in class. Take time to relax after. Make sure that you are giving yourself time to refocus and rejuvenate. Day by day, you will get through the year, and you will have grown in so many unexpected ways that you may just appreciate the challenge!

Benefits of Teaming with Families

Young children's learning and development are fundamentally connected to their families. To support and promote children's learning, early childhood programs need to involve families in their children's educational growth and invite families to participate in the program.

Partnering the home and school environments offers benefits for children, families, and classroom settings.

Benefits for the child include:

- **Enhanced self-image:** When a child sees family members working together with school staff, they have a tangible experience that validates the importance of their time and effort at school. Having family members partner with teaching staff communicates, "I am important enough that my mom/dad/grandmother will invest time with me here."

- **Better child-to-adult ratios:** The more adults that are partnered with children within the classroom, the more learning is facilitated. Channeling and coaching adults in the most effective format is key and will be presented later in the book. The egocentric developmental stages of early childhood bring a high need for attention. Just having another adult watching and encouraging children while they work brings great motivation for young children. Often, the intrinsic goal for a young child is more in the attention that he will receive, rather than in the academic goal he may achieve.

- **Increased opportunity for gaining literacy skills:** Families who help can bring more frequent interactions in literacy activities. Some examples are reading to a child, listening to a child tell a story, dictating oral stories into child-authored pieces, and modeling accurate articulation. Other examples include nurturing independence as a child begins to work independently with adult support, story comprehension through discussion, discussing solutions to problems (problem solving), and discovering details of text and illustration together. In addition to all of these benefits, families can help facilitate the incorporation of other curricular goals in math, science, and social studies into the given curriculum.

Benefits for Families

The following benefits are directly related to the success of the overall educational program within a classroom.

- **Taking teaching home:** A family who has been educated in supporting the growth of their child at school will hold the tools to foster teachable moments at home.

- **Enhanced self-image:** Family members too can develop a stronger self-image when family-child relational skills are fostered. Contributing to their child's education and their child's success brings rewarding intrinsic value. In addition, the experience gained by volunteering in a classroom provides excellent experience to list on a job application or résumé.

- **Increased school involvement:** A positive experience within their own child's classroom will likely build a family member's willingness and confidence to volunteer in broader ways within the school. By building skills of identifying decisions based on what is best for children within your classroom, you are empowering families to take this view to wider areas of influence.

- **Stronger parenting skills:** When a family member is coached to practice developmentally appropriate strategies, these attitudes can be taken home and applied there. When expectations are in alignment with a child's developmental stage, success can be found in both the child when he achieves it and in the adult when she facilitates it.

- **Enhanced communication:** By being in the classroom regularly, an adult can share family preferences, child needs, and any other circumstance that may be affecting a child's learning. An adult may also get questions about the educational goals or classroom expectations clarified immediately by being in the classroom setting.

Benefits for the Classroom

- **Families bring ownership.** Possibly the only other individuals as committed to the success of the children in your class are the children's own family members. Most are motivated for their child to succeed to the point that love of the child can fog an accurate view of their success and achievement. This is not a negative, for when we believe that a child can attain an expectation within developmentally appropriate markers, they most likely will. This provides a core strength and confidence that sometimes only a family member can inspire. Effectively channeling such highly motivated and passionate partnership with families will bring a more balanced and appropriate view of their own children's strengths and needed areas of growth.

- **Families bring effective resources.** Skills and interests of family members bring terrific learning opportunities. Some careers bring special aptitudes that can build on knowledge. For example, in addition to sharing the aspects of being on the job, a veterinarian can coach the class on good choices and appropriate care of classroom pets. Partner these resources throughout curricular goals during the year.

- **Families can support a balanced child-adult ratio.** As previously discussed, the more adults that can be partnered with children within the classroom, the more learning can be facilitated. The egocentric developmental stages of early childhood bring a high need for attention. Just having another adult watching and encouraging children while they work brings great motivation to young children.

- **Family culture can be incorporated.** Firsthand explanations and clarification of cultural diversities expand our understanding of each other. When we model acceptance and embrace those different from our own personal experiences, we are teaching in a powerful way.

Communication Home

The next pages are sample letters home providing information about encouragement, classroom management, and communication. Frequent communication with families keeps the partnering process moving forward.

Letter Home

What Every Child Needs to Know About Being a Good Kid

Dear Families,

Every child needs to hear encouragement on a regular basis. The more they hear how first-rate they are, the more they will believe and demonstrate just that!

Challenge yourself to incorporate some of the following compliments into daily exchanges with your child.

- You are wonderful!

- You are a great helper.

- You have such good ideas!

- You're a great person!

- I'm so lucky to be your mom/dad/grandma/brother!

- Thank you for trying so hard.

- Thank you for being patient.

- I'm sorry. (*It is so important that children realize that no one is perfect and we do not expect perfection from them.*)

- I like it when you help.

- Can we talk about it?

- You are a gift.

- You are special.

- I love you!

Sincerely,

Classroom Management Assessment

When children know what is expected of them, they fall into a positive rhythm of behavior where learning can take place. Respectful behavior enhances success!

Please help us! Read and then practice some of our classroom guidelines.

_____

_____

_____

_____

Help motivate your child with positive rewards for:

- good behavior
- taking turns
- being polite
- working together
- using classroom materials appropriately

Redirect distracting or disruptive behaviors by:

- offering reminders of the guidelines
- redirecting distracted activity to the task at hand
- giving gentle verbal reminders
- offering a slight change or modification of the activity
- offering another choice

Model positive life skills such as:

- good listening
- proper use of materials
- willingness to ask for help as needed
- the use of good manners words
- following directions
- desire to do work that reflects your personal best

Thank you for helping us build a positive community of friendship and learning!

Home Communications Log

Child's Name _____

Family Member/Guardian Name(s) _____

_____

Contact Information (e-mail address, cell phone number, home phone number)

_____

Date of Contact _____

Reason for Contact: (Social, Behavior, Academic, Family Involvement)

Notes:

_____

_____

_____

_____

_____

_____

- ✂ - - - - - - - - - - - - - - -

Another simple strategy is to write your reply to notes from home on that note. Family members can never be sure that their little one actually delivered the note to you. Offer quick feedback by returning the note with your added comments. For example, if a note reads, "James lost his teddy bear and had a tough time coming into school today," reply right on the note with a short comment like, "Thanks for letting us know. James told us all about his morning. He seemed relieved to talk about it and ended up having a day with lots of smiles."

Remember to make a copy of all notes for your records. This may alleviate any confusion later.